SPEEDING UP FAST CAPITALISM

CULTURES, JOBS, FAMILIES, SCHOOLS, BODIES

BEN AGGER

Paradigm Publishers

BOULDER • LONDON

Copyright © 2004 by Paradigm Publishers

Published in the United States by Paradigm Publishers, 3360 Mitchell Lane, Suite C, Boulder, Colorado 80301 USA.

Paradigm Publishers is the trade name of Birkenkamp & Company, LLC, Dean Birkenkamp, President and Publisher.

Library of Congress Cataloging-in-Publication Data

Agger, Ben.
Speeding up fast capitalism : cultures, jobs, families, schools, bodies / Ben Agger.
p. cm.
Includes bibliographical references and index.
ISBN 1-59451-032-6 (hardcover : alk. paper)—ISBN 1-59451-033-4 (pbk. : alk. paper)
1. Information society. 2. Time—Sociological aspects. 3. Self—Social aspects. I. Title.

HM851.A337 2004
303.48'4—dc22

2004002210

Printed and bound in the United States of America on acid-free paper that meets the standards of the American National Standard for Permanence of Paper for Printed Library Materials.

Designed and Typeset by Straight Creek Bookmakers.

09   08   07   06   05   04
5   4   3   2   1

Contents

iii

I hear voices from the past,
from the sixties,
when a seed was planted.
The voices are getting louder.

Preface

I had to be dragged into the twenty-first century kicking and screaming. I liked my dad's old Royal typewriter, and I thought that the Internet was overhyped. I dismissed people who extolled information and communication technologies as the latest generation of technological utopians. I didn't "get" that capitalism was bending the Internet to its purposes, much as it bent radio, television, movies—the culture industry.

A decade after I published *Fast Capitalism* in 1989, I began to theorize the Internet as an important moment of post-Fordist, postmodern capitalism. This act of theorizing needed not only to stress the enveloping, dominating characteristics of these phenomena but also to identify their dialectical potential for undoing the existing social order—what Petrini calls slow life. I realized that I had opened the way for this theorizing in my earlier book, which identified the flimsy boundary between texts and the world as an important topic for contemporary critical theory. I interpret this "deboundarying" as a cause of the decline of discourse. I hope that this decline can be reversed by writing books, such as this sequel to *Fast Capitalism,* that both belong to and address the public sphere.

Initially I approached Dean Birkenkamp about reissuing *Fast Capitalism* in a new edition. He patiently explained that second editions of recondite works don't fare well in the literary marketplace and instead he suggested writing a new take on fast capitalism, which has become faster since the late

1980s. I owe the idea for this book to Dean, who, as always, helps his authors shape their projects imaginatively. Working with Dean is like working with a trusted coauthor.

I am also grateful to Julie Kirsch for doing an outstanding copyedit of the manuscript.

Many of my insights are derived from the "everyday life" I share with Beth Anne, Sarah, and Oliver as we traverse the early twenty-first century. I vividly recall certain landmarks in our family life that influence the way I see things: Our trip to Paris; 9/11, when my kids were at school and learned of the events; the day I realized that my kids had stopped wanting to go McDonald's.. We all work hard to slow things down, recognizing that carefree childhood is a metaphor for, and an opening to, the good society.

1

Faster Capitalism?

The doorbell just rang. It was the mailman bringing a package from Amazon.com. In our suburb between Fort Worth and Dallas, good bookstores are hard to find. There is the obligatory Barnes & Noble outlet, where you can order a book with your cappuccino or calendar. But there is nothing in the way of an independent, intellectual bookstore of the kind we used to enjoy in Buffalo and nearby Ithaca. So we order from Amazon. Today's book is called *Wired to the World, Chained to the Home* by Canadian social scientist Penelope Gurstein (1991).

Canada figures in this story. One of my main themes is the way that distance (as opposed to immersion) affords clarity of vision. Here, distance is Canada. A host of Canadian scholars and writers, from Harold Innis, Marshall McLuhan, and George Grant to John O'Neill, Douglas Coupland, and Arthur Kroker have addressed the impact of rapid information and communication on self, society, and culture. McLuhan coined the term *global village* and Coupland the term *Generation X*. Perhaps Canadian theorists are well positioned to understand the inextricable connection between culture and power; after all, Canada exists in the shadow of America and yet it shuns superpower politics and identity. Canadians are also keenly aware of the importance of boundaries.

The other thing that happened today is that I finished writing *The Virtual Self* (2004), a book about the impact of the

1

Internet. Instead of sending a pulp copy of the manuscript to the publisher, I simply e-mailed files across the country. The publishing house is based in England, but it operates internationally. The book was signed and developed in the United States, typeset in India, and printed and bound in the United Kingdom. Virtuality is the question of the day, indeed of the year and perhaps of the decade. Critical social theorists are scrambling to make sense of new information technologies just as we use these technologies to order books and write them. *Speeding Up Fast Capitalism,* a sequel to *Fast Capitalism* (Agger 1989a) in light of the Internet, doesn't simply reflect the world but is implicated in that world. As I explain in *The Virtual Self,* I am not antitechnology or anti–information technology; I use technology, but it also uses me in ways that give me pause to consider it theoretically. I sometimes use a cell phone, fax machines, pagers, the television, of course, and courier services (the Amazon book), all of the accouterments of an industrial civilization that some call post-Fordist—beyond the era of Henry Ford's mass production. An excellent book on this post-Fordist world is Dyer-Witheford's *Cyber-Marx* (1999).

Capitalism, Time, and Boundaries

Fast capitalism is a term I coined in 1989 to describe a new stage of social development. The term has found its way into the theoretical discourse; recently, a scholar published a book with Princeton University Press using the term *fast capitalism* in the title (Holmes 2000). When I published *Fast Capitalism* with University of Illinois Press, I had just taken delivery of a computer in my faculty office at SUNY-Buffalo. I've been a typist since the eighth grade, and this IBM PC, as I recall, was a useful addition to my intellectual technology. But even in the late 1980s, as I thought through my argument about a new stage of capitalism called "fast," I could only dimly imagine

2

what was to come in the subsequent decade as the Internet and World Wide Web colonized the planet, changing the way we start our days (with e-mail), communicate (e-mail, again, and chat), learn about and teach the world (Web pages), entertain and stimulate ourselves, shop and travel, and make intellectual contacts. This book describes how a fast capitalism has gotten even faster, and it traces the implications of all this for culture, work, schooling, childhood, diet, and bodies. You don't have to be a social theorist to read this book productively. I will summarize and update the argument of my earlier book in this first chapter and then apply these insights to a host of human and social issues.

The key word in all this is *acceleration,* a term used by Douglas Coupland in the subtitle of his book *Generation X* (1991). The rate of communicating, writing, connecting, shopping, browsing, surfing, and working has increased since the Internet came on the scene. I was correct, in 1989, to notice that capitalism had sped up since Marx's time, and even since the post–World War II period in which the Frankfurt School theorists wrote about domination and the eclipse of reason (see Jay 1973; Wiggershaus 1994). But I didn't foresee the extent of acceleration and instantaneity we have come to know today. Who could have? What has happened with the Internet proves my earlier point about the ways in which *boundaries* of all sorts have been broken down, largely owing to the Internet, television, and what Doug Kellner (1995) calls media culture. As I will explore, perhaps the most crucial boundary under assault by the information technologies that stream through us is the boundary between personal and public life (see Sennett 1977). Nothing today is off limits to the culture industries and other industries that colonize not only our waking hours but also our dreaming.

As I argued in my earlier book, published fifteen years ago but separated from our world today by a vast gulf, I intend the adjective *fast* to modify "capitalism" in two ways. The first involves time and the way it is compressed as the pace of everyday life quickens in order to meet certain economic imperatives and to achieve social control; idle hands are the devil's workshop. The second involves erosion of boundaries, which are effaced by a social order bent on denying people private space and time. The two senses of the term are related. A key boundary separates personal and public life. Another key boundary is between the text, as I call all writing and figuring acts, and the world—society and culture. I was especially concerned to think about what I (Agger 1990) have called the decline of discourse (similar to Jacoby's [1987] last intellectuals) as a result of a postmodern capitalism in which texts are *dispersed* into the environment. They ooze out of their covers and become lives, reproducing the world—quickly—through a casual reading. Reading becomes casual because people have neither the time to read carefully nor the critical intellectual skills, which they are not provided in this educational milieu of standardized learning and accountability testing (see chapter 4 on schooling and childhood). Also, as I pursue in the next chapter, casual reading is conditioned by casual writing, which both reflects and reproduces people's lack of intellectual preparation to read the big books of yesteryear—Susan Sontag on photography or cancer, Lewis Mumford on the city, C. Wright Mills on the military-industrial complex, Sartre on existence and bad faith, Marcuse on one-dimensional consciousness.

In this sequel to my earlier book, I am interested in the activities of *boundarying* and the removing of boundaries, both of which are characteristic of a shift from early- and mid-twentieth-century capitalism to post–World War II and now early-twenty-first-century capitalism. What some people call postmodern capitalism involves removing boundaries between people and among social institutions heretofore viewed as separate, such as work and home. I argue for reboundarying where I contend that the self is at risk of losing her freedom and even her mind in a fast, and now faster, society of

4

information, communication, surveillance, and stimulation. But, as I contend in my final chapter, which ends with practical recommendations for selves, we cannot simply turn back the clock to an earlier era, the premodern, in which these invasive and accelerating technologies did not exist. (In fact, enslavement to the clock is part of our problem.) Many of the technologies I discuss are useful because they will deliver us from scarcity and poverty; they are also useful because they empower people to know and master their worlds. Think of the Internet, which has made the task of writing this book, among other things, easier. As I point out repeatedly in *Speeding Up Fast Capitalism,* whether technologies are bad or good depends on their uses, their context. The main context in which these faster technologies are used is capitalism, which thwarts the humanism for which I am arguing. Better to change capitalism than unplug the Internet (although changing capitalism will transform the Internet, and a transforming/transformed Internet will help change capitalism).

What underlies these two senses of the word "fast" in our stage of capitalism—acceleration and the erosion of boundaries—is what one might call *instantaneity.* This captures nicely the postmodern experience of the world. We expect things quickly, instantly, including our fast food, fast cars, fast bodies, fast work, fast reading, and fast writing. What better vehicle of instantaneity than the Internet? Although I composed much of my 1989 book on my trusty PC, which was provided to SUNY faculty because secretaries had been laid off and faculty were now expected to do their own typing, there was no Web, no surfing, no chat rooms. E-mail was restricted to universities. The Internet was initiated by the Defense Department to be a fallback communications system in the event of nuclear war. It was implemented by computer nerds at four major American universities as they got their mainframes talking to each other. It was a technology restricted to the military, government, and university. Today, it is a mass technology, available to most who live above the poverty line. I even see people who live in a local homeless shelter come to the university bookstore in Arlington in order to use free computers. My kids, born in 1991 and 1994, began to learn how to use computers in the second grade; they not only have classes in how to use computers but also take reading tests on their classroom and library computers, for which they need to know basic computer operating skills.

Instantaneity refers to the sheer speed of computers with high-speed Internet connections. When the Internet isn't overwhelmed by Saturday morning traffic, it hums, connecting one to Buffalo or Bulgaria in a few keystrokes. As I mentioned earlier, I e-mailed book chapters to an editor near Boston. We talked about the chapters a few minutes after I sent them. Instantaneity also refers to the human experience of accelerated information flows and the impact these have on the sensibilities of people. What I termed fast capitalism was fast by comparison to the slower world of my father, who grew up in Manhattan during the 1930s. He knew only radio, "regular" mail, newspapers, billboard advertising, train travel, the New York Giants and Brooklyn Dodgers. The faster capitalism of the 1980s, half a century later, was so different: television, express mail, fast magazines, electronic advertising, and jet travel, including the Concorde. And my dad's world was quicker by half than Marx's world of a hundred years earlier, when people rarely traveled, seldom read, and knew little of the world beyond their local scenes.

Social history and cultural analysis by decade are rarely reliable. But in the past ten years the world has sped up, especially communication and information, so that we can talk about a distinctively new experience of the world I am calling instantaneity, which has brought about another distinctly new experience called *globality*. We can connect with people anywhere, communicating with them and reading e-mail and their Web pages, without waiting long for a response. Time compresses and space shrinks when information and communication are accelerated.

6

The compression of time and space changes the experience of being human (see Harvey 1989). The self suddenly has no boundaries between itself and the world. One's home, time, and even thoughts are invaded as the virtual world streams through them. Instantaneity breaks down boundaries and barriers, bringing about a kind of dedifferentiation, which some say is the hallmark of postmodernity. Although I don't retract what I said in *Fast Capitalism* about how we still inhabit modernity (and capitalism), not postmodernity (and postcapitalism), the erasure of boundaries and barriers by media culture and information technologies is a distinctively new feature of human experience (see Huyssen 1986). As the world speeds up and compresses, producing the experiences of instantaneity and globality (see Hardt and Negri 2000), we lose the capacity for retreating into privacy in order to evaluate what is going on around us and to us. We lose the distance from the world required to assess it critically, marshaling the analysis and energy to change it. Instead, the self merges with the world, losing the boundaries surrounding what Freud originally called the ego.

This manipulation of experience takes us a stage beyond what the Frankfurt School called domination, which itself intensified what Marx termed exploitation or alienation (see Agger 1992b; Marcuse 1960). Now, the self experiences its own dissolution and dispersal as it is bombarded with culture, control, and commodities. Critical theorists talked about the eclipse of reason to capture this idea (Horkheimer 1974). But they assumed the possibility of critical distance from the world, and thus the integrity of the self, that makes critique and consciousness-raising possible. The Internet reduces this distance, drawing us so close to the world that we cannot find a standpoint from which to reflect or to engage in reasoning.

Exploitation/alienation was Marx's (1967) term for the theft of workers' surplus value, the basis of profit, in market capitalism. Alienation is a total human condition in which workers are separated from their work, its product, the working process, other people, and nature. It is in the "logic" of capitalism not to compensate workers for a part of their daily work time. Capitalism shrouds this theft of surplus value in the illusion of false necessity and permanence; the intellectual systems that create this veil are called ideologies. Marx published volume 1 of *Capital* in 1867 and he died in 1883. His first important work was composed in the same year that Charles Dickens published *A Christmas Carol.*

The Frankfurt School theorists and Lukács, a Hungarian Marxist, began, during the 1920s, to revise Marxist theory in order to explain why the socialist revolution that Marx expected failed to occur. They theorized that false consciousness, produced by ideology, had become more prevalent than Marx anticipated. Marx felt that economic crises would push workers to the brink of revolutionary action. But by the end of the Great Depression, in the early 1930s, it was evident that capitalism was more resilient than Marx allowed for. The "state" or government intervened in the economy, violating Adam Smith's strictures about the invisible hand, in order to forestall economic crises through Keynes's strategies of deficit spending and investment implemented by Franklin Delano Roosevelt during the first one hundred days of his presidency in 1932. And, as the Frankfurt School came to recognize, for example Horkheimer and Adorno in their (1972) book *Dialectic of Enlightenment,* the "culture industry" intervened to stave off people's psychic crises. It did this through entertainment, leisure, and a subtle, enveloping social philosophy of conformity and control. This social philosophy, deeply implanted in everyday life, was termed domination—a condition of deepened alienation impervious to straightforward critique or social criticism of the kind Marx composed. In a condition of domination, people develop what Marcuse in *One-Dimensional Man* (1964) called "false needs" for products far beyond their basic needs. Domination is characteristic of the "late" stage of capitalism between the 1930s and the 1970s, corresponding with the Fordist stage of capitalist development. The Fordist stage of capitalism, modeled on Henry Ford's social technologies of mass production, situates factories and warehouses full of inventory in big cities; production runs are long and relatively inflexible; labor unions are efficacious.

DISPERSED DISCOURSES/DECLINE OF DISCOURSE

After the 1970s, post-Fordist capitalism entered a new phase with the decline of unions and mass production, globalization, and the extensive use of automation and "flexible" information technologies such as the Internet. In this phase, which Jameson (1991) and Harvey (1989) have termed postmodern capitalism, all sorts of boundaries, especially between truth/falsehood, text/world, and private/public, began to collapse. As a result, institutional dedifferentiation has occurred, with institutions such as work and family, education and entertainment, merging into each other. There is much debate within social and cultural theory about whether this new stage is a genuine postmodernity, beyond an earlier modernity addressed by Marx, Weber, Parsons, and the Frankfurt School, or whether this is only a variation on capitalism that uses postmodern technologies and a postmodern media culture to deepen people's alienation. I take the latter point of view. In my work, I use postmodern insights to explore the discourses of fast capitalism, but I don't forget that our economic system is still based, as it was for Marx, on the private ownership of means of production and the bureaucratic coordination of work. But things have changed significantly since the mid-nineteenth century, particularly in this dedifferentiation of social institutions. The most important aspect of dedifferentiation is the invasion of home and even head by cultural imperatives delivered via advertising and the Internet. The Frankfurt School termed this "total administration," but they did not foresee the extent to which this would happen, with information technol-

9

ogies and media culture becoming more prevalent and more sophisticated than they were in the 1940s and 1950s, when the critical theorists focused their attention on radio and movies.

I have argued that it is useful to view "discourses" as having been dispersed into the everyday environment of work, home, school, even the body. A fast capitalism accelerates cultural messages and both work and family. Few writers write texts on important social topics that do not require doctoral training on the part of readers (think of the books of Sontag, Mumford, and Mills that I mentioned earlier). Writing is dispersed into the sentient world, taking the form of advertising, scripts, Internet chat, Web pages, romance novels, mass-market fiction, gossip magazines, and electronic 'zines. Even academic writing becomes formulaic, written to build careers and not to enlighten, engage, and enrage readers. In my late 1980s and early 1990s discussions of the decline of discourse, which I view as a central feature of fast capitalism, I focused on the eclipse of books, of writing and reading, that imperils the projects of critical theory and social analysis. Marx in the mid-nineteenth century took for granted that he and Engels, his friend and collaborator, could write straightforward works of social criticism, exhorting workers to commit the revolutionary deed, that would be read and understood by workers everywhere (see Marx and Engels 1967). "Workers of the world, unite!" Today, we can no longer presume that writers can write such books or that readers will read them. We cannot presume that publishers would publish them, given market pressures and intellectual stupefaction on the part of readers who prefer fast reads to slow and challenging ones.

That framework of analyzing alienation, domination, and the decline of discourse as a gradual deepening of false consciousness seemed compelling to me in the late 1980s. At the time I stressed, and I stress again, that my analysis recants neither Marx's criticisms of capitalism nor his utopian solutions—a society beyond class and the alienation of labor. However, I did not foresee the rate at which the decline and dispersal of discourse would accelerate with the Internet, which is an important new factor in a Frankfurt School–oriented analysis of cultural domination today. The Internet both changes things and makes them more the same. It does not overthrow capitalism, pushing us into postmodernity. Nor should it simply be demonized. We must theorize and analyze the Internet as an important aspect of what Marx originally called the mode of production, just as we recognize it is as a mode of cultural production and reproduction, producing selves much as it also spews forth and circulates commodities in the busy traffic of e-commerce.

MODE OF INFORMATION?

One year after I published *Fast Capitalism,* Mark Poster (1990) published a book in which he argued that we have surpassed Marx's nineteenth-century mode of production toward a symbolic economy that could be characterized as the "mode of information." When I first read the book, I thought he exaggerated the transformation of industrial technology into information technology. But he pointed to developments in technology and culture that fundamentally change the way we look at everyday life in the wired world and at social structures underpinning everyday life. *Speeding Up Fast Capitalism* examines those social structures of culture, work, family, childhood, school, the body, and diet from the perspective I outlined in my 1989 book. Like Poster, I remain a Marxist, although what it means to be a Marxist is at issue today, especially since the United States has moved far to the right, the labor movement is nearly dead, and there is no organized socialist opposition of any kind. Things are only somewhat more conducive to left-wing politics in England and Europe.

I don't deploy the concept of the mode of information, even though I agree with Poster that information technologies require critical theory to rethink some of its basic assumptions developed in a manufacturing stage of capitalism. I stress that the underlying structural feature of our society is still capitalist; I suggest that capitalism has accelerated, become global, dedifferentiated its institutions, and colonizes the self and everyday life through what Tim Luke (forthcoming) calls the vectors of virtualization. These are all topics of this book, which retains the framework of fast capitalism but assesses fast capitalism in light of the Internet and other accelerating, instantaneizing, dedifferentiating, deboundarying, and globalizing features of post-Fordism.

But my story will not be a totally dismal one, as the reader might suspect by having read this far. I disagree with the original Frankfurt School theorists that domination is a total ether suffocating every critical impulse, co-opting every subversive thought. Marcuse's notion of one-dimensionality and Horkheimer and Adorno's image of total administration were already overdrawn, although they had good reason to exaggerate their portrait of post-Holocaust capitalism, given the horrors of the death camps that made them wonder whether we had regressed behind the Enlightenment. They brilliantly argued that victorious capitalism adopted and adapted techniques of totalitarianism, albeit a totalitarianism sanitized for the suburbs. These include one-dimensional thinking, Marcuse's term for positivism, a fact fetishism that inures one to utopian possibilities and makes the present seem like a plenitude of social being. The Frankfurt School theorists argue that the ideology of bourgeois economic theory, which prevailed in Marx's stage of capitalism, has given way to an ideology of positivism, of "enlightenment," as Horkheimer and Adorno ironically call it, that reduces knowledge and discourse to sheer representation driven by scientific method.

The critique of representation has much in common with postmodernism's own critique of what Derrida (1976) calls the metaphysics of presence, as Ryan observes in his *Marxism and Deconstruction* (1982). Postmodernism is even more helpful than critical theory in focusing attention on discourse—the ways in which language and images entrap us by thwarting our imagination of a different, better world. The good life is reduced to goods, including name brands, the imaginary of advertising representing freedom and gratification in certain cars and running shoes. As post–World War II capitalism shifts from an ethic of savings to one of spending, especially with the mechanism of personal credit, cultural discourses produce consumption and selves, stimulating the economy and trapping people in the routines of their everyday lives.

In the last decade of the twentieth century I sought a discursive grounding of critical theory as I blended critical theory and postmodernism. The discursive turn in critical theory allows us to enrich the Frankfurt School's concept of domination, appropriate to the second stage of capitalism, by allowing us to trace domination or one-dimensionality to certain language games all the way from advertising to science. These languages games, as Wittgenstein explained, are the situated, context-bound ways in which people transact their lives, what the ethnomethodologist Garfinkel (1967) called practical reason. In this book, as I had begun to do in *Postponing the Postmodern* (2002) and *The Virtual Self,* I ground a postmodern critical theory in everyday discursive practices that allow us to view "domination" as language games out of which people can opt in favor of new games, new discourses, new lives, and thus new social and political institutions.

Key here is conceptualizing the self not as "subject," as the Frankfurt theorists did following Kant and Hegel, but as an active speaker, doer, actor who, as Sartre's existentialism recognized, is firmly grounded in existence, or everyday life in Husserl's phenomenological terms. Derrida helps us view the self both as reader and writer. Reading becomes a strong intervention into texts that are inherently opaque, "undecidable," to use Derrida's telling term. Thus, my account of the Internet will alternate between a Foucauldian and Adornian pessimism about literary grids of power and a Derridian and Marcusean optimism about how new sensibilities, virtual selves, can write their way out the imprisoning language games of positivism and domination, creating literary communities and a new culture using the nearly frictionless vehicle of the Internet. This will be a Marxist account only if we allow Marxism to be revised, which it must be because the early twenty-first century is significantly different from the late 1800s, when Marx composed his critique. Dickens's *Christmas Carol* is now a campy movie starring Bill Murray.

Why did capitalism speed up in the first place? Was it ever really slow? How fast can it get? (How fast is the speed of light?) Marx explained that production of commodities and consumption of those commodities must be matched. If shopping cannot keep pace with production, it is impossible to extract what he called surplus value from commodities and then to convert that into profit. Consider a Ford Explorer SUV sitting as inventory on a car lot. Many hours of human labor have been expended in fabricating this vehicle. Workers have been compensated with income and benefits; materials have been purchased; the factory must be kept operating; there is wastage; advertising campaigns are in place; the vehicles must be shipped to market; the dealership must be capitalized. In his great book *Capital,* Marx explained that the key to understanding the production of economic value is through an analysis of labor power and labor time. Workers toil long enough each day so that if they quit at, say, 3 p.m. the Explorer could be sold at a price sufficient to cover all of the above costs. But they are kept working on the line until 5 p.m. in order to transfer additional (or what Marx called surplus) value, conceived as labor through time, to the vehicle. Actually, with Henry Ford's assembly line, the worker does not make a single car but works on many cars. By 3 p.m., twenty SUVs may have been produced. By 5 p.m., an additional five SUVs may roll off the line. These five SUVs are an investment in steel, plant, advertising, shipping, and wages. If they linger on the car lot, they represent a cost to capital. But once they are purchased, for a grand total of about $150,000 or more, profit flows back into the coffers of the capitalist. According to Marx, workers who work these additional two hours of the working day are, strictly speaking, unwaged. They have worked sufficiently hard by 3 p.m. that if all the vehicles heretofore produced were sold, the owner of the plant would recoup his or her investment, including the cost of wages.

The extra two hours the workers work are called surplus labor time. That duration of working transfers enough value to the commodity (*x* number of Ford Explorers) that profit can be realized once the vehicles are sold. But if the vehicles languish at the dealership, they are merely an unprofitable investment, a dead weight. People must be stimulated to buy them. In Marx's and even Henry Ford's eras, people's needs were so basic that they didn't need to be told by advertising to shop. They bought bread, meat, milk, eggs when they could. They purchased drab clothing and coal for heating. Luxuries were unheard of, except for the very rich. Ford, with great insight, recognized that the assembly line could produce many cars, which, if they were affordable, would result in a huge volume of sales. Although the profit margin on each vehicle would be lower than on a handmade Rolls Royce, many more units would be sold. Although Ford used advertising, it was not until the mid-twentieth century that people needed to be told to buy more than one car and to trade in their cars every few years in order to acquire the latest, best design. These are what Marcuse called false needs.

In *One-Dimensional Man* Marcuse explored needs in 1960s America. He recognized that capitalism must stimulate demand lest the economy stagnate. Capitalism also must divert people from their alienation, which is an endemic feature of capitalism. Hence advertising and the consumer culture would stimulate needs far beyond the basic needs of the nineteenth century, let alone the ninth century. Marcuse's analysis builds on Marx's point that inventory is unproductive, failing to provide profit for the capitalist. The entrepreneur is supposedly entitled to profit because he took the risk of starting the business in the first place. At least that's what Adam Smith said in his 1776 book *The Wealth of Nations* (1998). But Marx morally disagreed: He felt that profit is owed directly to workers' unwaged labor time (the extra two hours, in my example above) after they have worked hard and long enough for the commodity to be sold at a break-even price. During these extra hours of labor time they are working for free, in effect doing volunteer work. Of course, this isn't voluntary; it is economic slavery: If they refused, they would be fired. And so my analysis of fast capitalism doesn't differ from Marx's original understanding of the exploitation of human labor but takes Marx's insight into the unproductiveness of inventory further, further than even Marcuse would have imagined, writing in the early 1960s.

Capitalism in the contemporary era needs to find ways to liquidate inventory, keeping people in the malls and show-rooms so that their shopping transforms inventory into profit. If they don't shop, the economy as a whole slows because individual firms and enterprises would not have the resources, absent sufficient cash flow, to continue to operate. Or at least the businesses would contract, laying off workers. This creates a vicious circle: Laid-off workers cannot spend, causing other firms to fail or contract, laying off additional workers. Eventually, there is widespread unemployment and a depression. This is an incendiary situation for capitalism, threatening revolution. Thus, shopping is all-important for the well-being of capitalism.

Henry Ford speeded up production using Durkheim's (1956) principles of division of labor and Weber's (1978) insights into bureaucratic organization. Mass production, which Ford initiated, depends on a large volume of production and slender profit margins so that consumers can afford cars, televisions, even prefabricated suburban homes. Ford brilliantly recognized that middle-class and even working-class Americans would drive cars if he priced his Model T affordably, accepting a small profit margin in return for mass sales. Ford's assembly line became the basis of virtually all subsequent social technologies of mass production, requiring specialized work stations and the constant rhythm of the line, which brings the product to the worker and not the other way around. Ford thus quickened the pace of production.

Faster production must be matched by faster consumption. This is the basic quandary of post–World War II capitalism, in which a puritan ethic of savings is replaced by an ethic of spending, aided by credit. Fast consumption depends on insatiable needs, on planned obsolescence, on striking the fancy of consumers increasingly inured to claims of The Next Big Thing. Marcuse once wrote that you could learn a great deal about American culture by watching an hour of television. This hour would need to include advertising for cleaning products, cars, running shoes, exercise equipment, diet aids, cosmetics, clothing, life insurance, even cemetery plots. The manufacture of taste by what Ewen (1976) called captains of consciousness is a requirement in fast capitalism. Once we can meet people's basic needs, at least for the 75 percent of Americans above the poverty line, we must produce false needs and thus "false" selves using the culture industry and a media culture.

By the end of the 1980s, advertising was omnipresent in our media culture. You could not watch a movie in a theater, view a football game on television, read a newspaper or magazine, or drive down the street without being enveloped by exhortations to consume. But since then, with the advent of the Internet, fast capitalism has quickened and become more seamless. The Internet is clearly a vehicle of advertising. More important, it is an electric circuit bridging production and consumption. You can shop from home, from your laptop, from your cell phone as we move from Henry Ford's era of mass production to a post-Fordist era of flexible production, suburban and international production sites, courier services that facilitate just-in-time manufacturing, and electronic shopping. Using the Internet, you can order products quickly and without burning fossil fuels by driving to the mall. You can order specialized products that aren't manufactured until you place your order. The era of cash purchasing is coming to a close as we use credit and debit cards. The Internet accelerates shopping and thus completes the circuit of production and consumption in ways unimagined even by the Frankfurt School, let alone Marx.

This change in how we shop not only quickens the pulse of the economy and connects production and consumption but also contributes to the process of de-urbanization and perhaps even the "de-malling" of America as people shop from home and the office and don't need to venture out into three-dimensional space in real time. The Internet has profound impact on shopping, producing, and the life of cities and suburbs.

The Internet also has impact on social institutions that used to be separate to some extent. The home is no longer a sheltered harbor but a point of production (for teleworkers, as Gurstein [1991] calls them) and consumption. The Frankfurt School theorists were concerned that the self (or subject, as they termed it) was being whittled down by political, economic, and cultural imperatives to conform and consume. The Internet dismantles barriers or boundaries between private and public, home and work, in ways that profoundly affect our identities and intimate lives. Whole families go online in order to check e-mail, visit chat rooms, and consume. My wife and I have shielded our young children from the Internet at home, removing temptation as well as danger. Our kids surf only when they accompany us to Internet cafés, where we allow them twenty-minute blocks of Web time. But their young friends visit chat rooms, where they assume screen names, shop, using parents' credit cards, and consult pornographic Web pages. In chapter 4, I consider the acceleration of childhood as a distinctive feature of a faster capitalism. The Internet is invasive, as are cell phones, pagers, fax machines, and, of course, television and radio. The self is at issue and at risk.

In my analysis I address the three stages of capitalism: that of Adam Smith and Marx, that of the Frankfurt School, and our postmodern stage, transformed by the Internet and media culture. But I don't want to portray the boundaries between these stages of capitalism as clean; one stage blends into the next. Capitalism has always assailed the self, first with alienation, then domination, and now the decline of discourse, which is accelerating in the early twenty-first century. Each stage preserves the negative features of the stage before it, which is why I consider my analysis Marxist. Our economic system is still capitalist; we still lack a public sphere in which people can debate ideas (or even have ideas); now, the dispersed texts of postmodern discourse itself have become a trap, an invasion of our privacy and identity. Daniel Bell (1973) first predicted a postindustrial civilization in which class conflict disappears and poverty and social problems melt away. This is an updating of Comte's, Durkheim's, and Weber's perspectives on the progressive rationalization of modernity, which culminates, at the end of history, not with the nineteenth-century factory system or even Henry Ford's Detroit automobile plant but with a technological elimination of work. Champions of the Internet, such as Negroponte (1996), drink deeply of this postindustrialized imagery of a society without factories, friction, or unions. But Bell was wrong: ideology hasn't ended, nor have capitalism, class struggle, and labor. Labor simply dons a different uniform—first blue collar, then white collar, then no collar, at least on casual Friday (see Braverman 1974; Mills 1951). The job site has metamorphosed from factory to office to home, even to the car, where you can grip the wheel with both hands and talk into a cellular earpiece as you coordinate your employees or build relationships with clients.

Does the Internet Change Things?

Celebrants of the Internet want to believe that clean, electronic work replaces forever the alienated labor of Marx's inhospitable factory, situated in Dickens's dark and dreary London. But work is still with us, if not the backbreaking toil of nineteenth-century sweatshops or coal mines. There are still factories and coal mines, but the factories are often sited outside of the United States, indeed outside of the industrialized West. They are out of sight and out of mind. And the office work that champions of the postindustrial society such as Bell extol is often as heavily coordinated, manipulated, and alienated as blue-collar work, especially where workers pursue not careers but jobs, which require little skill and lack a promotional ladder and union protection. Often these jobs—secretary, data-entry clerk, bank teller—are done by women, which makes them pink-collar workers. Renaming secretaries "executive assistants" doesn't overcome their powerlessness and low compensation.

The *Wall Street Journal* would have us believe that the Internet and e-commerce are delivering us from socialism. "Adventures in capitalism" is their current advertising slogan. But capitalism is a rough ride, not an adventure, for those who worry about the next paycheck, paying the mortgage or rent, saving for their kids' college educations, and paying the credit card bills. Almost everyone in America has these worries. The proclamation that we have surpassed Marxism and socialism, blue-collar work and unions, poverty and misery is premature (see Aronowitz 1992). Anxiety haunts America. People are anxious about their jobs and whether they can make ends meet. They are also anxious about the meaning of life, which is elusive in these materialistic times. Capitalism's production, via the culture industry, of needs that are in effect excessive or superfluous creates psychic stress for selves caught on an accelerating treadmill of working, shopping, debt, overeating, and dieting.

In this book I examine concrete ways in which a faster capitalism, accelerated by the Internet and media culture, manifests itself in people's everyday lives. I examine cultures, jobs, families, schooling and children, and bodies. All of these venues allow us to see the effects of acceleration, which has contradictory aspects. For example, people are torn between eating supersized french fries and losing weight before swimsuit season. Kids are exposed to a fast-paced standardized curriculum and accountability testing, yet they don't know much about society, culture, history, and values—the things that really matter. The family is an open window to the world, connected by the Internet and television, and yet the family is a shell of the nurturing environment idealized by the Victorians. The Internet affords us many cultural opportunities, but people read quickly and for escape and writers don't write challenging books.

I am describing a postmodern worldliness, dexterity with details. My daughter's classmates can talk about cars and popular culture, but they know next to nothing about religion, politics, and other cultures. They know the mall and its food court; they can surf and chat; they discuss blockbuster movies and videos. But they have no clue (to use a trope of the early twenty-first century) about the Vietnam War or the aftermath of the war in Iraq. They think everyone goes to church and that no one is an atheist. Racist and homophobic epithets trip off their tongues, and they think the boundary of the known world has the memorable shape of the state of Texas. They watch a lot of adult television; they play video games; and they "date" (with mommy driving them around). They are familiar with sports, and their college horizons include only in-state universities.

This dexterity with details and acquaintance with ephemera mark a fast capitalism that engulfs thought and reflection. Of course kids are but reflections of their parents, who, in early twenty-first-century America, run in place. This isn't a literary age, with reading and writing occupying people's days, unless you count e-mail, chatting, and gossipy magazines. Although religiosity is prevalent, it is a signifier of conservative political and social values, or, as a postmodernist might call it, a signifier of a certain race, class, and cultural differentiation from the Other—godless communism. Faith is fast, too, and equally superficial.

In our world, there is abundant concern with the self— career, grades, college preparation, gender identities, bodies— but little self-consciousness. People have many reasons, but they don't reason. The parents of my kids' friend prize what are called "activities," including soccer, baseball, piano lessons, and church groups. Activities consume time that could be spent in quiet contemplation, reading, writing in a diary, helping others. Volunteer work is done only for the sake of college applications and resumes. Bright kids are stigmatized by those more "normal." Dexterity with details and ephemera is highly valued, and bookishness is the curse of the nerd or geek.

Little of this is new. Babbitt abounds in American culture and history. Richard Hofstadter (1963) chronicled anti-intellectualism in America, identifying its salience and intractability. And the fast media of our culture compound anti-intellectualism by giving it the veneer of worldliness. Yet virtual selves are more parochial than their forebears; they know more about facts and trends, but they know less about what really matters. Sloterdijk (1987) has identified cynicism as the mindset of the postmodern person, and he has a point. Cynicism in fast culture combines a worldly assessment of costs and benefits with shallow materialism. Both have always existed, but they were leavened by church, literature, and even a relatively elevated political culture. Compared to the venal and opportunistic politicians of the present, FDR and Jimmy Carter are Gandhi and Martin Luther King. We get the politicians we deserve: Bush remains popular even though he has ruined the economy and launched a dangerous incursion into Iraq and a dubious war on terror.

I return to my argument in *Fast Capitalism*. There I noted that we have entered a stage of civilization in which texts ooze out of their covers and into the world, commanding attention by having their literary signatures removed. We don't read advertising as a text, nor television, nor Web pages. We certainly don't read science as poetry or fiction but as sheer representation, an impression promoted by science's busy concealment of its authorial heartbeat and literary signature. The word we give to these scientific cleansing procedures is *methodology,* which, if done artfully, lulls us into readings that automatically convert into lives. During the 1990s I argued that a critical or deconstructive program needs to identify the author of media culture, of science, of popular fiction, of newspapers, of all social texts. I hold to that. Now, a decade later, I notice that the Internet has the potential to colonize our lives further by bombarding us with messages and meaning. But the Internet is a curiously dialectical phenomenon in that surfing reveals the Internet to be a literary beehive, an engine of authorship and readership, especially where amateur pages are concerned. And e-mail is a daily ritual of composing oneself, of launching into prose and of connecting, which is a democratic and communitarian impulse. As I chronicle the speedup of an already quick capitalism in the pages that follow, I will also address the liberating potential of the Internet as it affords connection and fosters authorship and even citizenship.

One of Derrida's most important points is that reading writes. He means that every text, because it is undecidable—murky, deferring, question-begging—requires explication and interpretation. These literary activities are necessary strong interventions into the text. Think of reading Shakespeare or Marx, examples I pursue in the following chapter. Think of making sense of the State of the Union address or parsing a lyric by Nirvana. Derrida privileges reading because he notices that reading is a literary version in its own right, potentially even a text if it is published or posted. The Internet is a publishing house, allowing readers to write. It is a public sphere, if not a three-dimensional one. It is political, even if virtual politics only prepares the way for a more materialist politics. It can liberate the self to be an author, and then a citizen, in charge of his own life. The Internet can both enslave and enlighten.

A good Hegelian, Marx insisted that capitalism would negate itself and emerge in a higher order of being, a better society. For Marx, dialectical energy was to be found in the economy, split between capital and labor. The Internet is similarly dialectical, containing positive and negative aspects. It has an amateur, independent, edgy quality, allowing graduate students to post their work and offer explications of their intellectual heroes. I have found pages by professors, students, and citizens that are remarkably conversant with difficult traditions and texts. These pages clarify, criticize, extend. They are not mere hagiography or hero worship but creative contributions in their own right. Without the Internet, we simply wouldn't know about this work, these scribblings, these alternative perspectives until their authors were established comfortably as middle-aged academics. The Internet is also full of advertising, entrepreneurial pages, and pornography (it never seems to quit!). It can be mainstream or sidestream, orthodox or heterodox. Conservative institutions like banks and universities have cookie-cutter corporate pages. But alternative bands, alternative journals, and alternative intellectuals have Web pages too.

And e-mail and chat are dialectical. Millions of office workers begin and end their days by churning through their voluminous e-mail, answering, deleting, ignoring. I know of a rich celebrity and entrepreneur who sometimes has more than two thousand e-mails awaiting him in the morning. I'm told that he spends every morning doing nothing but answering those messages. I received an answer from this zillionaire to a request for advice and, yes, money to support an intellectual project. The response was composed in lower case, not to evoke e. e. cummings but because this guy's life is so hurried that he can't pause to depress the shift key. The answer was curt, and he couldn't bother to write his name in salutation but only a single initial, the letter m. Switch roles, though, and I can see his point: Thousands of chumps like me ask him for funding, unbidden. I often ignore crackpot e-mails and bulk mailings. Yet I pay attention to my e-mail because I frequently find nuggets of gold: people who write from Timbuktu to tell me that my work inspired them and asking if I could please clarify something I wrote. Before the Internet, I had little way of knowing my impact on the field or how many like-minded people there are out there.

Chatting is conducted synchronously, not asynchronously, as e-mail is. By synchronously I mean that we chat, in real time, corresponding with each other nearly instantaneously. But when one writes an e-mail one might receive an answer tomorrow, or next week, or never. I'm sure I'm not alone in having sent a significant e-mail, to a publisher or colleague for example, and anxiously awaited a response, checking my e-mail inbox compulsively. One quickly learns that a watched pot never boils! I am convinced that serendipity and surprise rule the Internet. Chatting, though, forces the issue and opens one to all sorts of interactional complexity. People don screen names and enter chat rooms, creating a persona that may or may not reflect their "real" persona. In *Life on the Screen* (1995), Sherry Turkle praises the Internet for allowing people to try out multiple personalities, almost therapeutically, enriching their everyday identities with fantasies and wish fulfillment. I suppose that may be true. But for someone with my perspective on fast capitalism, it is easier to view this as meaningless catharsis, a bleeding off of critical insight.

What I notice first about both e-mail and chat, as well as cell phone use, reading groups, coffee klatches, and hanging out, is that they answer to our need for sociability, for community. Seeking community via virtual chat is strange because, unless a picture is supplied, you are simply sending your thoughts into cyberspace and hoping for human reciprocity. Who are lonesomeindenver, hotlawyer, jeanius? The answer is that it doesn't matter if you are using chat to make a connection, to feel the virtual human touch and receive virtual recognition of your humanity. E-mail is less anonymous, especially if the user's email address is from an organization, business, or university and not simply from Hotmail or AOL. I know from his e-mail address that my correspondent is from Washington State University, the Arlington Independent School District, or the American Sociological Association. Although young people use Hotmail and Yahoo in the same way that chatters use screen names to conceal their identity, there is less purposeful deception with e-mail than in chat rooms. There is nothing inherently wrong with deception; it is interesting, because it is a utopian search for a different personality and perhaps even a different life. Life on the screen is necessarily different from life in the neighborhood, boardroom, or classroom.

CYBERSPACE: DEMOCRACY OR DOMINATION?

Since 1989, alienation has become more widespread. The pace has quickened and people are more stressed. They are more alone. The world is more dangerous, especially after September 11. There is growing economic anxiety. There is greater unemployment now than during the Clinton years. Classroom competition for college entry has redoubled as the size of the birth cohort grows and as the stakes rise: Good corporate and professional jobs spell a life on Easy Street, although, as it turns out, people on that track are harried and heartless, too busy to enjoy it all. Virtual selves experience a postmodern desperation borne of cynicism, worldliness, and the loss of home, neighborhood, even nation. As a result, they venture into cyberspace, seeking solace for wounds suffered in their "real" lives. Does cyberspace function merely as a placebo or can it make a difference, especially given the sprawling, chaotic, unplanned, amateur nature of the Internet? I address this question in my final chapter, after I examine the particular venues in which a fast capitalism has quickened over the last decade, largely because information and communication technologies like the Internet intrude into our everyday lives. As I discuss culture, work, family, school, childhood, and the body I explore contradictory tendencies in each case for both progress and regress, improvement and backsliding by the standards of Marxist humanism and feminism. As people are stressed and squeezed by the culture industries, they find ways of resisting, for example using the Internet as a counterNet, adopting healthier diets and lifestyles, tuning out the electronic prostheses streaming through us and our homes, resisting the speedup of childhood and education, and opposing bureaucracy and the division of labor in workplaces.

Theorists tend to portray postmodernity monochromatically, either as a betrayal of or a break with modernity and progress. The picture is more mixed than that, with regressive and progressive moments coexisting fitfully. Although a faster capitalism solidifies domination and makes it even more difficult to name than it was for the Frankfurt School, accelerating capitalism brings it closer to its demise, assuming that Marx was correct to view capitalism as a contradictory system necessarily undoing itself by concentrating and centralizing wealth. Marx was correct, in my view, to regard capitalism as impermanent. Yet scientific Marxists, beginning with Engels, Kautsky, and Lenin, have given the impression that Marx was a positivist who preordained socialist progress in the very laws that he composed to describe capital's laws of motion. But, as French existential-phenomenological Marxist Maurice Merleau-Ponty eloquently cautioned, "the date of the revolution is written on no wall, nor inscribed in any metaphysical heaven" (1964a: p. 81). The revolution, if we can sustain that imagery at all in these cynical times, is a contingent event depending on the collective will of virtual selves who use cyberspace as the equivalent of a New England town meeting, the public square outside the Winter Palace in St. Petersburg, or the free-speech area on the Berkeley campus in which Mario Savio and other New Leftists railed against the university's complicity with the military-industrial complex. Cyberspace is also Big Brother, a site of surveillance and social control.

In *The Virtual Self* I prepared the way for this discussion of an accelerated capitalism by considering the impact of the Internet on self, society, and culture. Here I go further and address the Internet's role in fast capitalism as it hastens—and also opposes—the decline of discourse. My previous book focused on self, identity, and everyday life. This book engages social structures, albeit sometimes virtual ones. I ended *The Virtual Self* with the image of readers writing their way out of domination, using the public-access forum of cyberspace. I retain that prospect here, although I ground the resistance and rebellion of virtual selves in particular venues such as culture, work, family, schooling, childhood, and bodies. I consider the Internet here as a means and medium of acceleration, but I don't restrict my analysis to information technology. I consider offices, homes, classrooms, bodies, and food. These are not texts nor topics of a cultural studies that avoids materialist concerns. But texts matter because they are matter; they compel lives by appearing to be forces of nature—handbooks of operating procedures, marriage manuals, school books, diet and exercise guides. In fast capitalism, as I noticed a decade ago, the texts that matter in our lives become lives because they are read without pause, quickly, without ontological questioning about first principles, definitions of definitions, grounding assumptions.

Cosmetics advertising assumes the pursuit of body beautiful, cast in heterosexual terms. Personnel policies and operating procedures assume that the needs of the organization trump human needs. Social studies textbooks assume that we can tell a linear, progressive narrative of the history of the

United States or the world. Marriage manuals reproduce male dominance in the family by accepting the gendered division of labor, with men playing instrumental roles and women intuitive roles. Marcuse portrayed an industrial civilization in which we don't dig beneath these texts, and the practices they both describe and recommend, for their hidden assumptions about the nature of being. One-dimensional society denies philosophy as a lived practice, as a way of being human by asking the question of its question. The more capitalism accelerates, the less people pause to treat these texts, and the lives they recommend, deconstructively, engaging their blind spots and biases, their politics and passion, their perspective and position. In one-dimensional society the epistemology in use is positivist; facts are worshipped, and they are stripped of their history and their possible undoing. Today the facts have gotten faster. As Marxists, the Frankfurt School theorists wanted to restore dialectical thinking, which, as Marcuse indicates in the second preface to his study of Hegel, *Reason and Revolution* (1960), is negative thinking, thought that negates the merely apparent—facts, data. Negative thinking thaws the frozen data of social science and positivist culture into molten chunks of history, of position and negation, leading to a higher synthesis.

This is heady talk at a time when poor people and people of color don't vote, when white men vote Republican and white women are split between the two parties; when people run up huge credit card debts; when parents pay so that their kids can play on "select" sports teams; when people waste money and ruin their health overeating and then try to burn off the calories and fat with expensive fitness-club memberships and fad diets. False consciousness prevails, if by false we mean that people don't think for themselves but allow the culture to do their thinking for them. Marx had this right: The ruling class enforces its ideas so that its power won't be challenged. This is the basic principle connecting the three stages of capitalism. However, since the nineteenth century, ideological texts have been dispersed into the landscape, appearing to be figures of nature and not authored acts. Billboards, Web pages, magazine and television advertisements, school textbooks, science, evangelical religion, and patriotism that sells flags and decals all call forth conformist behavior and uncritical thinking.

In 1989 I sought "critique's community," a notion of inter-personal relations, a public sphere and a common culture in which people could read deconstructively and think negative-ly while working for change in their everyday lives. My aim in 2004 is no different, although there may be a new vehicle of this consciousness-raising, critical thinking, and community organizing—the Internet. Transition from the slow pulp era to the fast electronic one, even as the pulp era was quickening by the 1980s, augurs certain efficiencies in political action. To be sure, a virtual politics is not necessarily transforming unless it shakes power in Congress or parliament and in boardrooms and banks. I tend to view the Internet as prolegomenon, a preparation for both local and global political action but not their completion. Yet we cannot simply ignore the frictionless, inexpensive Internet as a vehicle for touching people and reeducating them just because the Internet is also a vehicle for corporate culture and commerce.

The Internet allows culture and its imperatives to consume and conform, to stream through us, but at the same time the Internet elicits the author in us, first as reader and then as writer. Say you get sick but not sick enough to see a doctor. You might use a search engine to search for your symptoms and find various pages that help you figure things out. You then either see a doctor and hope to get the relevant medi-cine or you treat yourself. My wife, kids, and I have done this on several occasions and we found ourselves "empowered" by this self-care. No one is denying that medicinal amateurism can be dangerous if you get crackpot Internet advice or you misinterpret a complicated medical page written for doctors. But the Internet, by facilitating self-care and self-education, narrows the gap between amateur and expert, between lay-person and professional, between client and provider. The professional establishments resent this, cautioning patients to see a doctor first. But smart and inquisitive readers can save themselves time, money, and anxiety by investigating their symptoms on the Web and then acting accordingly, including sometimes seeking medical attention. I learned more about how to treat my tennis elbow on the Web than by visiting a doctor who didn't specialize in sports medicine. Once one is injured, activity frequently trumps inactivity because it facili-tates healing if done in moderation. And the stretching and icing I learned from the Web were far more ameliorating than were the things the doctor told me to do, including not playing tennis. I also cracked the code of cure in a "slow" way, consulting a college tennis player who advised me to loosen my strings, after which I got well quickly.

A faster (and a slower) capitalism, thus, facilitates parapro-fessionalism and amateurism, all the way to self-care. Capital-ism thwarts self-reliance because, as the Frankfurt School well understood, it wants to reduce the self's efficacy in order to make it more pliant. The Internet makes resistance possible, beginning with the first Google search for information, advice, analysis, and contact information for experts, support groups, and chat rooms. The able reader interprets a jumble of infor-mation and advice and becomes a writer if and when she sends e-mails, enters chat rooms, or perhaps even puts up her own page on the topic at hand. As I neared fifty, I looked forward to my first colonoscopy with trepidation. I found research-based medical pages that I couldn't understand; I found medical pages with easy-to-follow frequently asked ques-tions; and I found a few pages put up by knowledgeable amateurs counseling people like me to have colonoscopies without fear. I remember one page of this kind put up by a very intelligent amateur, which had a lot of credibility with me. Armed with information about what to expect as well as photographs of the procedure itself, I had the colonoscopy done, without much discomfort; a half hour spent on the Web helped me learn about the procedure and become more comfortable with the idea of having it. As a result I have advised all of my friends to have colonoscopies.

Reading Web pages on colonoscopies and colon cancer and sharing the information with your friends won't overthrow capitalism. But it demonstrates an empowering that threatens both slow and fast capitalism: The self is no longer a passive victim but involves herself in her own cure, and in curing others, which could be a revolutionary metaphor. Reading converts into writing, and potentially into political action, when one shares one's insights with others. An enduring component of capitalist ideology, in all its phases, is the experience of being passive, of being a victim. The Internet allows ingress into the lives and cures of others. The American Medical Association cannot control this, nor can hospitals. Instead of allowing your family doctor to refer you to a gastroenterologist, who performs a colonoscopy without your knowing much about what is going on, the Internet helps you, the patient, take control of your own treatment. Some of my friends didn't have a colonoscopy when they turned fifty because they were told by their family doctors that they didn't need one. (There are different perspectives on such matters, perhaps influenced by the cost-cutting strategies of insurance companies.) But my reading on colon cancer suggests that these doctors are wrong, that colonoscopies not only detect colon cancer but, even more important, also prevent it by allowing the medical specialist to identify and then remove potentially cancerous polyps from the colon, which can't be detected and addressed without this crucial procedure. In such cases, fast capitalism can be slowed down.

Marcuse spoke of a generalized condition of domination that he called one-dimensional thought. This condition has been deepened by media culture and the Internet in the forty years since he published his diagnosis. It can also be reversed through literary activities that use the media and Internet to educate and enlighten. These information technologies thwart ideology and slow down our everyday lives by giving us pause. Reading a challenging book or a Web page focuses attention and requires us to think the issues through. The Internet accelerates the pace of everyday life to the point that things blur and we become confused and compliant. But, as my examples demonstrate, it can slow down everyday experience, affording us the time and critical distance with which to make sense of the social structures conditioning us. The Internet can help us do social science and social theory. This is an important beginning; otherwise we succumb to the quickened pace of a life that appears to be entirely determined, an outcome of social fate and social nature.

2

Domination at the Speed of Light

In *Fast Capitalism* (1989a), I argued that public writing, indeed books generally, are eclipsed as the boundary between text and world fades. I suggested that books are dispersed into the sentient environment as secret writing—advertising, television shows, movie scripts, even the methodological gestures littering the academic science page. These are "gestures" that signify meaning, but they are increasingly difficult to read as texts, as authorial statements. Although books can still be found at Barnes & Noble and Amazon.com, for the most part these are quick reads, composed rapidly, and not considered tomes that stimulate thought and challenge the imagination. Such books of yesteryear aren't being written and don't get published for reasons that have much to do with a postmodern fast capitalism, including changes in the publishing industry, the decline of independent bookstores, and the growth of universities with their obscure codes. Writers can't sustain independent literary careers and so they turn to the culture industry or become tenured professors in order to make ends meet.

This was my argument in *The Decline of Discourse* (1990), which followed from my book about fast capitalism. Both of these treatments were provoked by lectures at SUNY-Buffalo during the mid-1980s by Russell Jacoby, one of Marcuse's most prolific and interesting American graduate students. In 1987, Jacoby published a book drawn from these lectures entitled *The Last Intellectuals: American Culture in the Age of Academe*. This was an exploration of American intellectual history that addressed what I was terming the decline of discourse—the inability of writers to write broad-gauged public books for educated readers who don't possess Ph.D.s, or even any degrees. Jacoby helped me think about writing, including my own, in structural and institutional ways, linking the decline of urban bohemia, the vertical integration of publishing houses and the professionalization of academic writing to a kind of intellectual decline, what he and Max Horkheimer called the "eclipse of reason."

Jacoby and I wanted to reverse this eclipse, first by understanding it. We didn't spare ourselves self-criticism for writing dense theory read by hundreds, not hundreds of thousands. He was purer than I was at the time because I held an academic job, indeed a tenured one. Jacoby was barred from academia, even though he had published prodigiously, because he was a left-wing iconoclast with a ponytail, labeled "difficult" by the organization men and women who frequently serve as department chairs and deans. Jacoby lived off his writing; he was putting his money where his mouth was. *Fast Capitalism* was my own attempt to think through the eclipse of reason using categories developed by Marx and the Frankfurt School, inflected by certain postmodern notions about discourse and the text. I felt that the Frankfurt School's critical theory has tended to ignore what French postmodern thinkers call discourse, which is especially strange given that Horkheimer and Adorno coined the term "culture industry" in their book *Dialectic of Enlightenment* (1972). So my book linked the Frankfurt School interest in cultural domination with the French emphasis on the literary subject who is positioned by discourses such as advertising, romance fiction, and science. I tried to understand the text, as the French called it, as a world, even if the world isn't all textuality.

Derrida once wrote that the text has no outside, that there is nothing beyond it (1976). This has been much misunderstood as idealism or solipsism: the world is one big library, without a material underpinning. Derrida didn't mean this, though. He was saying that you cannot stand outside of time and place and reflect the world (or text) perfectly using a certain representational language, especially that of science. Thus, every text is somewhat murky, "undecidable," as he termed it. The act of reading, therefore, is a strong literary intervention into the sense and sentience of the text, an act of sense making, of interpolation that takes poetic license in providing missing sense and meaning. Derrida helps us understand that readers, although initially disempowered, can become writers as they supply missing sense to texts that tend to "deconstruct" or unravel as readers probe them.

Postmodern theory helps us understand that the hierarchy of writer over reader can be undermined, indeed is always already undermined, by readers who, in effect, write their own versions of what they are reading. Take Shakespeare's plays. For the last four hundred years, people have been debating their meanings. Readers will continue to do so, given the indeterminacy of Shakespeare's texts. Or take the writings of Karl Marx, which, on the surface, appear to be scientific and precise. Are there two Marxes, early versus late? Was Marx an economic determinist? How did he envisage getting from capitalism to communism? Must the revolution be violent? Who would rule after the revolution? (For contrasting answers to these questions, see Althusser 1970 and O'Neill 1972). These questions are begged by Marx's texts, and they will remain forever unresolved. Postmodern theory empowers readers to author what they read, undoing the decline of discourse if they, too, enjoy access to print or pixels.

When I was composing my blending of postmodernism and critical theory in order to understand the decline of discourse, I couldn't imagine how the empowering of readers could transcend possibility and become actuality. Indeed, Jacoby suggested that publishing houses are less willing to issue "big" books on "big" topics, especially when written by learned amateurs. But in the intervening decade, the Internet has changed all this. It is now possible for amateurs and professionals alike to post their works and wares for all the world to read and view. The limited audience for an academic book can now burgeon into a vast audience for Web pages composed artfully and thoughtfully. Conduct a Google search for interpretations of Shakespeare or Marx and the list of interesting sites (a two-dimensional version of citations, also called cites) runs for many pages. There are thousands of entries, not all composed by professors. And these entries span the globe, with some composed in other languages that can be readily translated by the Internet browser software itself. Electronic publishing and publicity reverse the decline of discourse by opening up new venues for displaying one's work, beyond or the beneath the radar of commercial and academic publishing houses.

Academics worry about quality control. If anyone can post work on the Internet, how are we to ensure that bad work is filtered out? There are no guarantees, just as there are no real guarantees within academic journal and book publishing. Quality is in the eye of the beholder, here many beholders. I would argue that quality control is actually enhanced by Web publishing and posting, where one can be reasonably certain that one's work will be considered by thousands, whereas in academic publishing one's article or book manuscript may have been vetted by only a few readers in the field. Academics could respond that these are expert readers who have inherent credibility. But, as Linda Brodkey argued, "academic writing [is] a social practice" (1987) conducted in language games and interpretive communities that implicitly favor certain styles of work. The kind of reading you get in academia depends on who your expert readers are. If they favor your perspective, you are likely to get published; if they reject your perspective, for example, if they hate postmodernism or critical theory, you will be rejected not for value-free reasons of "quality" but because their language games (worldviews) and yours are incommensurable. Every theory writer, indeed, as Norman Mailer (2003) points out in his autobiographical book on writing and writers' lives, every novelist, knows that he will be praised by some as brilliant and derided by others as pathetic. There is no pure marketplace of ideas, as John Stuart Mill hoped, any more than there is a pure economic market, as Adam Smith believed. Every reading is always freighted with the passion, politics, and position of the reader, who, when she reviews a work, becomes a writer (who needs to be reviewed in turn).

FAST WRITING, FASTER READING

There are two contradictory—better, dialectical—trends afoot. Writers write more quickly than ever, more sloppily, more formulaically as the pace of the culture industry accelerates. This occasions casual, carefree reading that almost always misses the point. On the other hand—a source of hope—the Internet can restore the public sphere by allowing many access to publicity and allowing readers to become writers, fulfilling Derrida's promise of social change. I have identified the dialectical nature of the Internet and other information technologies, which accelerate capitalism but also perhaps undermine it. Fast books can become public books, and hence political ones, if authors and their readership have a critical, political sensibility, capable of what Adorno (1973) and Marcuse called negative thinking. In this section, I explore the downside of the Internet, its acceleration of the rate of discourse's decline. In the following section, I examine the Internet's dialectical potential for self-negation, for becoming a medium not of acceleration but of critical distance and even political organizing.

At issue is not only the Internet but also the ensemble of cultural practices and discourses of what the Frankfurt School in the 1940s originally termed the culture industry. Radio, television, journalism, movies, mass-market fiction and nonfiction books, even academic textbooks and scientific journals precede the Internet and quicken the pace of culture. These media substitute for traditional slow pulp publishing whereby learned authors wrote books slowly for learned readers concerned with issues of morality, mortality, justice, and inequality. These are the books and plays that were written for most of human history, until capitalism cheapened publishing and popular culture, mechanically reproducing it for the many and not just the few.

The mass production of culture paralleled the mass production of automobiles and refrigerators, spearheaded by Henry Ford and his slender profit margins but massive output, using the assembly line's minute division of labor and pace. As capitalism survived the Depression and was strengthened by World War II, people had more time and money to spend during their "leisure." As Marcuse argued in *Eros and Civilization* (1955), capitalism needed people to spend their leisure time spending, both to keep the economy humming and to divert them from political rebellion. Cultural commodities like televisions and magazines were perfectly suited to newfound prosperity because they created profit and they distracted people, lulling them into the deep sleep of conformist thinking and political apathy. This is precisely how reason was "eclipsed," in Horkheimer's terms. "Domination" is the existential condition of being powerless, preventing powerless people from understanding its causes. It is a deepening of capitalist ideology that is no longer only falsehood but now also a sedative, a diversion.

The Frankfurt School recognized that capitalism could now mass produce ideology, both to reap profit and to immobilize. It did this through the entertainments of popular culture, which, like all culture, is a literary production. Although the Frankfurt School didn't use the term "discourse," which was an artifact of postmodernism, they understood domination as a discursive outcome, a positioning of literary subjects vis-à-vis literary texts treated as objects, as naturelike and, hence, as irrefutable. These cultural objects include advertising, music, fiction, and science. A fast capitalism, faster even than the capitalism of the 1940s, when the Frankfurt School conceived the concept of the culture industry, removes all traces of authorship, as texts ooze out of their covers and seep into the world itself, appearing to be inert pieces of nature and not rhetorical vehicles of political exhortation. This is as far as I got in my 1989 book, *Fast Capitalism.*

In the meantime, the Internet has achieved instantaneity, the nearly frictionless global transmission of meanings and messages, that is the latest stage of domination. We can watch the Iraq war in real time on CNN, transmitted by "embedded" journalists on the front line; we can view and hear live sporting events and pornography; we can chat with a global audience whose screen names conceal their real identities (if they even have "real" identities any longer). And the Internet reaches into our homes and psyches in a more thoroughgoing way than even the domination of the culture industry between the 1930s and the 1980s did. We live, instantly, the images we experience on television and the Internet, as instantaneity, as I am calling it, removes altogether the Hegelian experience of mediation—thinking things through, reflecting on one's life, reasoning. The lives scripted and depicted for us become our lives as we shop, dress, eat, vote, and talk mimetically, reproducing the lives and discourses of people who appear on our screens. Television and the Internet aren't ideological in the old-fashioned sense of making arguments about why this is the best of all possible worlds; they portray the present world as inevitable, and as desirable, inundating us with images and texts that seem to have no outside and that never seem to quit.

Postmodern experience is, above all, devoid of mediation, which is eliminated by instantaneity. Texts become lives by being lived, enacted by those of us for whom possibility is exhausted by situation comedies, cosmetics and clothing advertising, chat rooms. In a recent campaign, J.C. Penny depicted a dippy blonde lounging with her dippy boyfriend or husband, hearing a voice that intoned "You've got to have the fashions you crave!" and then telling him "I'm going shopping." This craving, this identification with the stylized people (always thin and always dippy) portrayed in our media culture, is the absence of mediation, which would hear a different voice. That voice would ask, "Is my credit card balance too high for more shopping?" "Do I really need these new clothes?" "What's wrong with me that I'm so suggestible?" "What does my life lack, other than a new pair of sandals or capri pants?"

That voice has been nearly muted as the postmodern experience of instantaneity prevails. People are worldly; they know how to shop, travel, network, strategize. They know more than their parents about ephemera, but less about what really matters. They don't experience culture as a series of arguments, borne of texts. Instead, culture inheres in the world, as solid and naturelike as buildings and glaciers. As capitalism quickens, people lose all distance from the world, which envelops them, capturing their sensibilities. The Frankfurt School called this domination, but they didn't foresee the extent to which capitalism would quicken the reproduction of meaning by dispersing texts into social nature.

Recently (November 10, 2003), the *Dallas Morning News* ran a front-page story about a new daily newspaper, called *Quick*, designed for young professionals in the eighteen-to-thirty-four age group, "an audience that's in a hurry." *Quick* will have synopses of articles from the regular slow newspaper, just the right length for people who are running short of time. The author of the *Dallas Morning News* story comments, "That group is always on the run" and is "a very difficult market to reach." This accelerated presentation will "help them manage their lives better and make better decisions and connect with people," according to the publisher.

Fast writing, thus, is matched by faster reading, which skips over words, sentences, sense. The deauthoring of texts is redoubled by reading that doesn't mediate (Hegel's term, again), meditate, or hesitate. Neoconservatives lament the decline of values, especially morality. They talk of the decline of cultural literacy, referring to younger generations who don't know the Bill of Rights or *Romeo and Juliet*. I choose to view this as the decline of literary skills under sway of electronic instantaneity and an accelerated culture industry. People watch too much television; they don't read enough; and when they read, they aren't challenged to think twice. No amount of K–12 standardized testing of children's interpretive abilities will remedy the blight of cursory reading, which is less a technical problem of the inability to pry hidden meanings out of a thicket of prose than a general inability to see the literary forest for the trees, reading metaphorically and analogically. I have never heard of a standardized test for metaphorical ability, allusion, indirection, and subtlety, even at the college level. Ours is a literal culture, a hallmark of positivism that confuses factual and conceptual knowledge. The decline of discourse involves the decline of metaphor and analogy, a crucial component of a nonliteral epistemology, indeed of literacy.

A GLOBAL AMERICA

When I wrote *Fast Capitalism,* I couldn't foresee the quickening of an already accelerating culture industry, and thus the further diminution of reason, with the aid of the Internet and other electronic prostheses. I didn't fully understand the relationship between instantaneity and globality. The whole world is becoming America, as Baudrillard (1988) once implied, because we export CNN, McDonald's, professional sports, rock and roll, Hollywood. We not only export information, values, and culture but also colonize the world economically, capturing new markets and expanding the reach of extractive industries. Globality is both a state of mind and an economic reality. It is also increasingly a military reality, as the U.S. government returns to the doctrine of Manifest Destiny in order to defend American economic interests, notably our access to oil. The decline of discourse is not local but increasingly global, reducing the world to a singular capitalism and its corresponding culture industry.

Difference persists, to be sure. In the Middle East, wars and terrorism rage over difference. Islamic fundamentalism is a regressive force, turning the clock back to premodernity. This is not to deny that progress has regressive moments, too, as Horkheimer and Adorno well understood in *Dialectic of Enlightenment*. Indeed, the commingling of progress and regress, under the banner of a world-historical reason, spells progress's eventual decline into catastrophe, from the Holocaust to September 11. The Frankfurt School argued that enlightenment needed to shed its hubris, its arrogance, toward the Other, the object, nature, and not pretend that it can understand everything and then master it. Adorno's post–World War II image of utopia was the redemption of nature, although this is nearly nothing compared to Marx's more robust image of a society of praxis. Adorno is pointing out that, after Auschwitz, it is disingenuous to pretend that progress hasn't been irrevocably tainted by its own regressive tendencies, the Nazis having used "rational" principles of scientific management and Fordism in order to produce mass death.

Adorno understood that the Enlightenment drives to replace difference with sameness, exclusion with identity. The global imperialism of American capitalism and culture is merely a moment in a larger process of civilization, literally of civilizing. The problem is that the civilizing forces, science and capitalism, are not without blind spots and dogma. A global America, facilitated by a quickened capitalism and its information and entertainment technologies, is not universal in the sense that Hegel required total knowledge to be. It is fragmentary, partial, perspective-ridden. Baseball's "World" Series is conducted between only U.S. teams. Soccer is the world's sport, by far, but in America it is a niche pastime at best. Hamburgers don't answer to a global appetite that preceded advertising; nor do SUVs and other examples of American automotive and technological arrogance. A global America substitutes the particular for the general, life in Topeka for life in Tokyo, which rapidly is coming to resemble Topeka.

The American decline of discourse, with fast food and fast culture, is imitated on a global scale, even though pockets of resistance and nonidentity remain, especially off the beaten path. America is imitated because it is affluent, by world standards, and because American political democracy, although a hollow shell of a more substantive democracy, is the envy of people subjected to despotism, especially of the religious variety. There is no denying that America stands for enlightenment and reason, for freedom from myth and tyranny. But it also stands for a rapacious capitalism; it is a country without guaranteed health care or child care, and it is one that despoils its environment and the environments of others. It is a nation with deep-seated race and ethnic hatred. It has a shallow media culture that prizes celebrity over substance.

It is important to disentangle America from modernity, or at least the potential of modernity, notably freedom from tyranny and from poverty. Although America is modern in certain respects, with a republican form of democracy and a vast industrial potential, it is premodern in other respects, with atavistic racism and pockets of both urban and rural poverty. Cities are unsafe and crime-ridden. People use alcohol and drugs in copious quantities. The younger generation of nonwhite urban dwellers is ill-educated, hopeless, and largely unemployed. As I explore in the following chapter, some people enjoy careers, with the prospect of advancement and decent compensation; others have jobs or McJobs (Coupland 1991) that barely keep them alive; still others have no work at all. Scandinavian countries, by contrast, are superbly educated and cultured. Their citizens enjoy universal health care and freedom from poverty. Their governments are progressive, pacifist, and noncolonizing. But Scandinavia doesn't export culture, or cultural illiteracy, because it occupies a more marginal role in the ethos of modernity, especially the chapter written by, and about, Henry Ford and his contribution to the era of mass production.

Modernity has gotten confused with America because America has played a major role in capitalist development and its globalization. It has also played a major role in developing democratic political institutions, even if these institutions are routinely undermined by economic and social inequalities that make republicanism a hollow shell. In this context, the global spread of Americana, from McDonald's to Madison Avenue and from CNN to courier services, is easily confused with what Habermas calls the project of modernity. This project, the possibility of which was inaugurated by the Enlightenment in the seventeenth century, includes reason, democracy, freedom from want, an end to war and violence, tolerance, and toleration—perpetual peace, as Kant termed it. Habermas argues convincingly that the project of modernity is worth retaining and hasn't been fulfilled, sociological claims to the contrary notwithstanding. In this (see, for example, his book *The Philosophical Discourse of Modernity* [1987a]), Habermas distances himself from neoconservatives, who equate modernity and America, and from postmodernists, who reject the project of modernity as overreaching and arrogant. For further development of Habermas's perspective on modernity, refracted through his reflections on 9/11, see Borradori's *Philosophy in a Time of Terror* (2003), which also presents Derrida's views on the topic.

I side with Habermas on these points, even though I question his critique of Marx's and the original Frankfurt School's optimism about reconstituting science, technology, and nature itself. This is not to deny that postmodernism can contain an appreciation of modernity that regards contemporary capitalist civilization, and its American epicenter, as in fact premodern, stopping short of full rationality and justice. Much of my own work has attempted to strengthen critical theory with insights from postmodernism, especially where the role of discourse is concerned. I have argued that fulfilling the project of modernity will entail moving a stage beyond what passes for modernity today, ending what Marx called prehistory. In other words, one can use postmodern insights to understand modernity's delay, the arrival of which could be called postmodern in the same sense Marx said that communism would end prehistory and initiate history. In my concluding chapter, I characterize the fulfillment of Habermas's "project of modernity" as the inauguration of *slowmodernity.*

One of the features of the project of modernity is totality, as Hegel called it, or globality. Although Habermas, postmodernists, and I would insist that regions, nations, and cultures need not be seen as developing along a singular, linear path to the end of history (or rather, with Marx, to its beginning), it is important that all societies and cultures develop democracy and a democratic public sphere, eliminate economic inequality, and end prejudice and discrimination. It matters little what we call this terminus—slowmodernity, as I propose, or communism or utopia. Habermas, although sympathetic with Marxism and first-generation critical theory, opts for "modernity," although in this he risks conflating what exists, for example a global America, and what is possible but as yet unrealized, notably a world in which America's hegemony has been ended. This prospect may be difficult for Americans to accept, especially where American Manifest Destiny has been so deeply ingrained in our political culture.

PULP TO PIXELS

Postmodernists such as Lyotard (1984) recoil when they hear words such as "progress" and the stories of modernity's unfolding in which they are embedded. They reject such "grand" or large stories as authoritarian, citing numerous examples of human atrocities committed in their name, from the Crusades to Stalin's camps. But we need such words, or the concepts underlying them, in order to make political and moral distinctions between bad and good, or at least between bad and worse. It is crucial to adopt a distancing posture above the fray in order to make such distinctions and issue such evaluations, even as we recognize that these are not absolute judgments unsullied by our standpoint or perspective. Postmodernism misunderstands the standpoint from which Marx did his judging, and existentialism too, as a privileged positivist vantage from which one can be as definitive as the natural sciences. In other words, as I have demonstrated, it is possible to read (better, to write) a nonpositivist Marx who rejected the reflection theory of truth but not the concept of truth.

For us to talk about modernity, progress, and reason we need to use a dialectical discourse, one attuned to its own blind spots, biases, and embodiment. Just because we recognize that truth is a matter of perspective doesn't mean that we shouldn't pursue it, especially where the alternative is to accept the present ("facts") as eternity. The impossibility of pure objectivity doesn't relegate us to subjectivity; it simply requires correctives to truth telling, especially an acknowledgment by writing of its inherent inadequacy, its question-begging, its deferral, as Derrida called it, of ultimate meaning. Habermas has attempted to reground critical theory in communication, which, he argues, provides an ethics and normative standard for critical theory, particularly in the implicit intention of speakers to reach an understanding and to abide by the power of the stronger argument. This is an effective response to postmodernist cynicism about grand narratives that aim too high and exempt themselves from the charge of being ideological. But Habermas restricts communication largely to interpersonal speech. He ignores larger cultural discourses such as fiction, film, art, and advertising, the sorts of topics addressed by cultural studies, influenced by critical theory, postmodernism, and Gramsci.

In *Cultural Studies as Critical Theory* (Agger 1992a) I explored the politics of cultural discourse. It is crucial to understand how positivism, identified by the Frankfurt School as a fact-fetishizing ideology in late capitalism ("one-dimensional thought"), used to be a *doctrine* of scientific epistemology but has now, in what I term fast capitalism, become a *discourse,* a way of talking, writing, and figuring the world. Domination is discourse, produced and reproduced in culture and everyday life. Adorno, Horkheimer, and Marcuse stopped short of understanding positivist domination this way because they did not theorize texts and writing in the way that postmodernists do. I have argued that we can't readily understand domination in an accelerated capitalism unless we theorize the dissolving boundary between texts and the world, which allows books to become lives, quickly. Books are no longer the considered tomes that started revolutions and authorized dictatorships; instead, they are fast texts written quickly and read even more quickly by consumers who don't actually read in a sustained and systematic way but merely peruse, the mien of the casual shopper strolling through the aisles of a chain bookstore. Books are sampled, like clothing at the Gap or Old Navy, sometimes discarded and sometimes selected. They may litter one's house or car in the same way that furniture and objets d'art do; they are decorative, and they are sampled when the mood strikes.

Critical theorists haven't fully understood the erosion of this boundary because they theorize "culture" as a monolith, an ensemble of nearly impenetrable texts and works. Wittgenstein, Husserl, Derrida, and Foucault help us understand culture as a textual practice, an accomplishment by situated speakers, readers, and writers who inhabit language games, life worlds, interpretive communities, and subject positions from which they compose their worlds. Understanding culture as textual practice, and as textual interpretation, is crucial for making political sense of what Marx originally called ideology as ideology is accelerated, transformed, and concealed in a fast—and then a faster—capitalism in which, in effect, *the author, and hence argument, is concealed*. In *Cultural Studies as Critical Theory*, my premise was that ideological domination in now achieved by "secret writing," especially through advertising and positivist social science that produce cultural and textual artifacts appearing to be pieces of nature, unalterable, pregiven, and, hence, ontological. These secret writings command lives because they are lives in the sense that they flow out of their covers and into the world itself, triggering instantaneous readings that become lives.

For example, we quickly "read" advertising, even absorbing it subliminally, that converts our desire, which is always thwarted in capitalism, into shopping. Clever campaigns have an almost physical hold over us, positioning us to get in our cars and drive to the mall. Today, in a faster capitalism, they compel us to log onto our computers and order products online, either through retail outlets or discount sites such as Ebay. We may view the advertisements while we are online as they pop up unbidden or they obtrude from the margins of sites we are visiting, wrapping themselves around our concentrated thought, which then dissolves into questioning about whether we should take advantage of the latest bargain in travel or pornography.

Communication via pixels is not only faster than pulp but also potentially more invasive, a vector of virtuality slicing into our work time, our home time, our very psyches. With television, even when it is treated as background noise, there is more resistance in using the technology: You have to turn it on and off. Although you can do other things while watching, to be entertained you have to fix your attention on the show, even if for only half an hour. Although televisions have been miniaturized, watching cable and satellite television tethers you to the screen. The Internet presents less resistance; it is anytime/anywhere. It can be accessed from desktop, kitchen countertop, laptop, even cell phone. It is both synchronous and asynchronous, allowing time and space to flex.

Domination occurs at the speed of light as capitalism accelerates, thanks to information and entertainment technologies such as the Internet. This is partly a matter of acceleration, instantaneity as I have called it, and partly a decoupling of time and place; domination is now a free-floating property of cultural discourses that insinuate themselves into every nook and cranny of existence and experience. As we move from pulp to pixels, texts lose their three-dimensionality and thus their somewhat secure mooring in time and space, such as in libraries and bookstores. In a quickening capitalism after the invention of television but before the Internet, this secure mooring was already imperiled; as I said in my earlier book, texts had begun to flow out of their covers and into everyday existence. By the twenty-first century, this process of dispersal, of what might better be called the dematerialization of writing, has been accelerated by information technologies that surround us temporally and physically. We therefore need to develop new concepts to understand what I am calling *dematerialization,* a key feature of accelerated/intensified/displaced domination in a faster capitalism.

DEMATERIALIZATION SPEEDS UP TIME, INTENSIFIES THE READER'S RESPONSE, AND DISPLACES DISCOURSE

An even faster capitalism than the one I addressed fifteen years ago not only deepens but transforms domination. Deepening is accompanied by transformation, which, as I contend in my concluding chapter, suggests new strategies of emancipation and suggests that domination today is not total, even though it appears to be more enveloping than it did even to Adorno, Horkheimer, and Marcuse. This is a fundamental paradox of a quickened capitalism: What seems to be the impregnability of domination is dialectically its own undoing if people learn to use information technologies to liberate themselves from both images and practices of domination.

Before we get to that point of possible unraveling and reconstruction, I want to consider the uniqueness of a faster capitalism under the rubric of "dematerialization," which describes what happens to texts and discourses as they are disseminated now with pixels. Of course, books with covers are still published, even though, as I argued earlier, they are not the same kind of books authored by Marx and C. Wright Mills. They are quick reads, insubstantial, not life-changing or earth-shattering. But the tendency of texts and books to be dispersed, as I called it, into the sentient environment has been accelerated and transformed in such a way that we need to revisit the relationship between texts, discourse, and culture, on the one hand, and society, on the other.

Dematerialization of discourse has three features, the *acceleration, intensification,* and *further displacement* of writing. The Internet fosters this dematerialization, although cell phones, faxes, and pagers also play roles. This process was set in motion sometime after World War II, as the culture industries created false needs and false consciousness. The Frankfurt School described this hegemony and generality of false needs/false consciousness as domination, a process that takes an intellectual toll in the inability to read and write. My argument here is that the Internet and other information, production, and entertainment technologies since the late 1980s have deepened domination but also, paradoxically, have made domination more vulnerable to grassroots resistance and transformation.

I am not suggesting a technological determinism because, with Marx and the Frankfurt School, I understand technology to be an ensemble of social relationships that frame our interactions with other people and with nature. The Internet didn't suddenly come out of nowhere to transform and deepen domination in a faster capitalism; it arose out of specific interests, which happened to be military and academic, in nearly instantaneous and global communication not reliant on fixed mainframe computers. And the Internet became a public phe-

51

nomenon, and broadly available, only when the computer chip was miniaturized in order to get astronauts to and from the moon during the 1960s and 1970s. Technology, society, and the self interact and intermingle in ways that blur the boundaries among them.

Accelerating, intensifying, and further displacing writing has the effect of cutting off texts' ties to the author. Instead, texts appear to be planets floating out into space, unconnected, except invisibly, to a literary epicenter, around which they orbit. Even before the Internet became a public literary and cultural tool, these three factors constituting what I am calling writing's dematerialization (admittedly an awkward term) had been set in motion. Television (Adorno 1954; Bourdieu 1998; Miller 1988), radio (Adorno 1945), movies (Ryan and Kellner 1988), corporate publishing, and even academic writing, as Jacoby tells us, were speeding up the literary process, intensifying the experience of cultural consumption, and displacing the author.

Think of going to a movie since the 1950s. Movie plots have picked up speed, jump cutting from scene to scene in order to keep (and subsequently diminish) the audience's attention. Television attenuated people's attention, requiring scriptwriters and producers to work doubly hard to be entertaining. A laconic pace spelled audience lethargy, which is bad for business. In addition, sitting in a large theater, gazing up at a huge screen with surround sound, has become an intensified experience in comparison to silent movies and especially to live theater, whose protagonists are merely life-sized. Today we are engulfed by the movie, which seems to be taking place not only in front of us but also inside our heads. There is no distance between us and the film, the distance that Adorno and his colleagues said must exist for people to evaluate what they are seeing and living. Finally, if the movie is cleverly made, we forget, or never even realize, that it is a simulation of reality, derived from a written script. There is authenticity, a lifelike experience of the film, that isn't effaced when the credits roll by quickly at the end, crediting a producer, director, and, yes, even a scriptwriter or team of them.

We experience the movie as the world itself, which fills us with meaning for two reasons. First, our lives tend to be more humdrum than the exciting lives led by Harrison Ford, Mel Gibson, and Gwyneth Paltrow. Movies enrich us, as does any good fiction, with missing meaning. Second, we fasten onto favorite actors and actresses, and we identify with them even as they shed one role and take on another.

The movie appears to be a piece of nature, obtruding into the environment as a chain movie house with a familiar contour and an advertising marquee that announces current offerings, with various ratings for objectionable content. This suggests that we "always" had movies and will "always" have them. Once inside, sitting in our comfortable seats in a darkened theater, we experience the advertisements before the main show, suggesting that we are watching television, though it is a more intense version of television in that the movie fills us with its enormity, sequencing, sound, emotional intensity, and heroic identification. Even if we linger to view the credits at the end, it doesn't occur to us that the movie, a vehicle for intensity and identification, was a text authored by someone or by committee. It appears to have been a natural stimulant, a way of enduring time on the weekend or evening understood as "leisure." The time was "worth it" because we had to shell out $6 or more for the ticket and perhaps $20 for the popcorn and drinks. I would argue that slow and fast capitalism blend: The movie's intensity and naturelike quality are matched by its commodity form, which is necessary for us to experience the movie as having been "worth it."

Movies belong to a slower capitalism, my dad's world of the 1930s, to a fast capitalism of my childhood and adolescence during the 1960s, and now to an even more accelerated phase in which culture has been hastened, intensified, and authorially displaced. As such, it is difficult to recognize the secret, silent arguments being made for one state of affairs over another. This is the power of dispersed writing, characteristic of a fast and now faster capitalism. When texts disguise themselves and their arguments, they argue all the more forcefully.

Horkheimer and Adorno make this case about the Enlightenment and its scientific method: By pretending absolute objectivity, science is all the more partisan, even if this partisanship is disguised as dispassion. Today, culture is positivist in the sense that it pretends to be a piece of nature, the movie theaters and chain bookstores littering our landscape alongside malls and fast-food franchises. These theaters are not beehives of busy textuality, with amateurs making and showing their filmic productions, but corporate chains that commodify their products and cleanse them of the appearance of authoriality—of having-been-written. This disperses directors' arguments, leaving the impression that cinematic vehicles accurately reflect not only the status quo but eternal necessity.

Film *becomes* an accurate reflection by being viewed and lived by unsuspecting subjects positioned by the theater chains as receptacles of the celluloid images appearing to be inherent in nature, not in argument or in a script. This is not exactly a conspiracy: The point of Hollywood film is to make millions of dollars, not to indoctrinate. Indoctrination, an antique term from an earlier, slower capitalism, happens as a by-product of a quick capitalism in which *pace* translates into *perception,* a way of seeing. Perception slides into action where viewers dress and talk like their filmic heroes. And these heroes are not composed in isolation from the larger culture. They dress, act, and talk like other members of the culture, twenty-somethings who have typical aspirations, values, discourse, style. Quickly, a vicious circle is described as culture both reflects and reproduces the quotidian world, the world flickering on our screens and in our mirrors, as we mimic our culture heroes (and they in turn mimic us, the "us" positioned by the dominant culture).

Marx originally made the point that culture flows from the pens of people who stand to make a profit from it, notably the ruling class or bourgeoisie. This is still true. But capitalism contains within it the mechanism of acceleration, so that people produce and consume faster. Although individual entrepreneurs can retire once they make their fortunes, they tend not to do so because they are also consumers, mortgaged to the hilt in order to enjoy the lifestyles of the rich and famous. It is crucial to remember that in capitalism people play multiple roles, not only working but also shopping, parenting, educating, eating, and exercising. Gordon (2004) calls this "complex personhood." Although the vastly rich can buy anything they want, they also invest on many fronts, requiring them to expand their businesses, and hence their capital, to pay off interest on loans that they need in order to make new investments. Although occasionally the rich retire (Ted Turner just did, apparently unhappy with the management of AOL since it merged with Time Warner), more often they continue working, shopping, and borrowing, never content with what they have. And the more they "have," the less time they possess.

Capitalism resembles a treadmill. You have to work extra hard just to keep up; eventually, the machine triumphs, and you are too exhausted to continue. The metaphor is imperfect because at least on a real treadmill you lose weight! In capitalism, if you can't keep up, you risk bankruptcy, job loss, ruin. Think of the dark storyline of *It's a Wonderful Life,* everyone's favorite Christmas movie. Jimmy Stewart's character is faced with the closing of his beloved building and loan and also with a prison sentence. He wants to commit suicide, until an angel intervenes to show him how rich his life already is. He gets back on the treadmill.

Capitalism has gotten faster since Marx's and Dickens's time, since Jimmy Stewart's heartwarming movie made in the late 1940s, since my childhood and adolescence in the 1960s, since I was thirty-seven, when I published *Fast Capitalism.*

Life has sped up because capitalism compels people to work harder, earn more, spend more, take more risks. It compensates them for all this with intensified leisure and recreation, especially consuming culture that does not require thought but can be absorbed immediately. Television meets a need for sedation following a long workday (or a boring day spent at home). It is also a perfect medium for advertising, which is entertaining in its own right. The Internet fills much the same needs, although it has more variety and invites the user to participate by typing in commands. I don't want to overdraw this distinction between a television capitalism and its Internet successor. They are both fast, although one is faster than the other. Both answer to the needs for more rapid spending and more intense escape and stimulation.

Marx and even the Frankfurt School felt that capitalism could be slowed by understanding it. This understanding would be derived from books of social criticism and theory, such as Marx and Engels's *The Communist Manifesto* (1967). This assumed a literary vantage, from which people could write unaffected by the whirling media culture that utterly reduces the difference between culture and society, thought and action. It also assumed a vantage from which readers could read with insight, patience, and self-reflection. Over the past decade, continuing a process set in motion with the origin of capitalism and its need for ideology and false consciousness, these vantages have been largely removed, with writers strapped into academic chairs, from which they perpetuate obscurantism, and corporate chairs, from which they script mainstream cultural vehicles such as movies, television, and advertising. Readers have been stupefied by reality television, voyeuristic tabloid newspapers and magazines, and the homogeneous selections of chain bookstores. And writers who don't have tenure cannot ignore these trends; they, too, succumb and write for a mass market, which almost always means writing down.

One cultural commodity between covers seems to be like any other; they all promise to be life changing, and hence none is. Publishers need "product," and writers provide it. Even university presses feel the economic pressure to turn a profit, and they publish fast books for a trade audience. Books of all sorts are losing their relevance, swamped by electronic cultural stimuli that fill every waking (and sleeping) hour with channels, programs, Web pages, and chat rooms. Although such activities are necessarily literary, their literariness doesn't bracket out the world in order to gain perspective on it but drinks deeply of the world, so deeply that it drowns in the ephemeral.

Rematerializing Writing, Slowing Down Domination

The genie of dematerialization, as I am calling domination accelerated to the speed of light, is out of the bottle and cannot be captured. Texts flow and ooze everywhere, defying their recognition as considered arguments, which they always are. The Internet drives domination to warp speed, filling up children's after-school hours with AOL chat and their parents' work and evening hours with e-mail and Web surfing. Satellite dishes and cable television make television background noise. Movies are enveloping total experiences. Bookstores sell everything but books. Is this genie demonic? Must the technology be destroyed?

I share Marx's view that technologies are best viewed as congealed, dead labor that can either liberate or enslave living labor. They can do so by shortening the workday or further fragmenting and intensifying back- and mind-breaking toil. Whether technology will benefit or hinder depends on the economic system in which it is located. In a utopia, whether we call it communism or the information superhighway, technology, like science, can answer to vital human needs for mastering, building, and knowing the universe, which need not be conducted in positivist, Fordist ways. In other words, the Internet can accelerate domination to the speed of light or it can slow it down to a crawl, even reversing it, as people use information, entertainment, and productive technologies for civilizing, humanizing purposes.

I am especially interested in the Internet as a means of amateur publicity, democratic consensus building, political organizing, and countercorporate culture. Although people who are wired run the risk of working and shopping around the clock, losing all privacy and self-determination, they can use the technologies of information and culture to project themselves outward, writing and talking beyond the established grids of power. I recently received a "blog" from a noted critical theorist about the war in Iraq, with suppressed information about the conduct of the war, casualties, and collateral damage. The Department of Homeland Security didn't censor this communiqué, and it has received wide circulation. Earlier, the same intellectual posted his book-in-progress about September 11 and the terror wars in Afghanistan, advancing the argument that the Taliban, which sheltered and aided bin Laden, was abetting terrorism against American icons such as the World Trade Center and the Pentagon using military technologies the United States gave to them a generation ago to fend off the Soviet Union. This is called "blowback."

In my concluding chapter, I suggest ways of slowing down a faster capitalism, even using its own tools and technologies against it. Instantaneity, acceleration, intensification, and displacement cut both ways, entwining or illuminating. This is the fateful dialectic of technology that offers hope that technologies such as the Internet admit of different, even contradictory, uses and meanings. Acceleration can be slowed down, indeed it slows itself down as it transports us so quickly that we suddenly see ourselves and the world from a distance, where before we were so immersed in the world that we were nearly indistinct from it. I am having this precise experience as I compose this book about an accelerating capitalism using the accelerated tools of composing that, even ten years ago, were slower and more cumbersome. I am writing furiously, thinking quickly, theorizing the technologies that envelop us in a world that seems to have no outside but that help us project ourselves so far above the ground that we can suddenly recognize ourselves down below. We recognize that, by thinking and writing hard, we can imprint ourselves on technologies that otherwise invade us as secret writing composed by authors and committees who don't have our best interests at heart.

3

The Omnipresence of Work

The Internet has had a major impact on the ways we work, our time, the family, private life, and accountability. The changes I discuss in this chapter all occur under post-Fordism, which moves us beyond Henry Ford's urban factory with its downtown warehouse, unions, mass production for mass markets, inflexibility of product lines, impermeable national boundaries, Taylorist scientific management, top-down authority, and rigid corporate culture. Post-Fordism is the economic engine and organizational framework of a fast postmodern capitalism, which has been accelerated by information technologies. Although the Frankfurt School theorists wrote into the 1960s, much of what we now called post-Fordism had yet to occur. Nor had the Internet been invented.

Postindustrial society theorists such as Daniel Bell augured a society beyond backbreaking toil, class structure polarized between capitalists and workers, long workdays and workweeks, short vacations, and bureaucratic authority. In *The Coming of Post-Industrial Society* (1973), Bell portrays the capitalism of his day as nearing a postindustrial cornucopia of goods and services and the resulting eclipse of class conflict. I wrote this once before, and Bell sent me a note chastising me for exposing him as a neoconservative. Bell used to be a socialist, but he recanted and moved to the right. This has been embarrassing to him. It is embarrassing, I suspect, because his predictions have not come to pass. Since

then, real incomes (that is, controlling for inflation) have declined. Poverty has become more, not less, prevalent while
corporate executives are paid many millions a year (strictly
speaking, they pay themselves, as we saw in the Enron scan-
dal).

People work more hours than they did even twenty years
ago. In the postindustrial society work was supposed to melt
away. However, even though we don't yet inhabit a society
beyond work and factories and maybe never will, the industrial system of Henry Ford and Frederick Taylor has been
surpassed, with production, now decentralized, taken out of
the urban core and rendered more flexible with shorter production runs. Workers don white collars, not blue; on casual
Friday, they may wear no collar at all. It is important to
theorize the continuities and discontinuities between the factory system of Marx, the assembly line and time-and-motion
studies of Ford and Taylor, and the present mode of capitalism in which people order products and even meals using the
Internet, engage in telework from home (or anywhere they
can lug their laptops), and enjoy a higher standard of living
than that of a hundred years ago, and even than that of their
parents. This is a confusing picture only if we forget that our
economy is still capitalist and that capitalism has proven more
resilient than Marx expected.

Saying this does not mean that Marx was wrong to identify
a central contradiction in capitalism between the private ownership of the means of production and the interests of labor,
of working people. Marx brilliantly recognized that capitalism
was self-contradictory, to use Hegel's language, in that its
strengths are also potentially its weaknesses. Capitalism can
amass great wealth and move civilization forward, further away
from misery and scarcity, but to do so it must exploit a whole
class of people, indeed the vast majority of people. This
exploitation cannot be forever concealed from workers who,
one day, will wake up and see what is happening to them,
especially if they have worked their ways through *The*

Communist Manifesto and other revolutionary tracts, perhaps including *Fast Capitalism!* Capitalism is especially at risk when its economy goes bad and people experience job loss, which isn't supposed to happen in Adam Smith's free market.

Marx recognized that the single greatest problem faced by capitalism is unemployment. Unemployed workers do not consume at the same levels as they had when they had jobs, thus causing firms to cut back on production and requiring additional workers to be laid off. In addition, the prospect of unemployment also nudges workers toward the revolutionary deed, especially when they learn that layoffs are not a natural law of our economy but an artifact of the free market, of government policy, of hard-hearted employers, of free trade, of outsourcing.

In this chapter, I discuss three aspects of the acceleration and transformation of work from the middle of the twentieth century to the early-twenty-first:

1. the introduction of telework, where people work from home using computers and telephones;
2. changes in time use, where people spend more hours than ever at work and doing work; and
3. the increase of low-end service jobs, in contrast to white-collar professional jobs.

TELEWORK

Gurstein (1991) published one of the first studies of telework or telecommuting, which she defines as work done at home and off-site, typically by women. It is done with computer hookups, telephones, and fax machines. On the surface, it appears to facilitate workers, again especially women, who are responsible for children and for housework. In some respects, the image of working at home in a leisurely way, without the corporate uniform, without a clock, and without a boss peering over one's shoulder, is consistent with the postindustrial utopia. Work, which used to be drudgelike and dangerous in the nineteenth-century factory and even in the twentieth-century coal mine, is now safe and comfortable. Above all, it is discretionary in the sense that homeworkers can pick it up and drop it at will, given the inherent flexibility of their time.

There are benefits to flexible working arrangements like this. Mothers (and fathers, too) can take care of young children and work when the children nap. People who don't like the regimentation of office life and corporate culture can work at home or at a neighborhood work site. Telework affords flexibility of time and place. But there are negatives. Being out of the office loop blocks careers. It can be lonely; it is clear that people work in order to find community as well as a paycheck. It may be difficult for some to have the boundaries between work and home blurred. The sight of a dirty kitchen may get in the way of productive work. And work problems may sully a pristine home life, preventing people from getting away from it all. That lack of compartmentalization is one of the hallmarks of a faster capitalism.

Companies benefit by, in effect, outsourcing work, freeing them up from having to provide infrastructure, such as office space. They may also save on wages and benefits. And they can reduce their on-site child care facilities for working parents who engage in telework and thus double as daycare providers. These economic benefits to companies are rarely passed on to employees, especially those at home. Companies save in both capital and human capital when they induce people to "office" at home or at Starbucks.

Teleworking, which tends to blur the work/home boundary, usually takes place at home. Another way to blur these boundaries and enable workers to have a life and kids as well as work is to implant "home" in the workplace. On-site company day care is one example of this. The Japanese lead the way in providing other aspects of "home" in the workplace, such as gymnasia, stores, and restaurants. But these accouter-

63

ments of the private sphere don't transform the workplace as much as working at home changes the home and family, turning them into points of production. For most of human history, especially in medieval agricultural communities, the home has also been a workshop, with every member of the family participating in animal husbandry, raising crops, cooking, cleaning, and caring for and educating children. Telework returns work to the homestead, from which it emerged during industrialization.

It would be more ambitious to implant home in office because it would humanize the office in ways unimaginable to Weber. Marx, especially in his early writings, talked about the humanization of work, although he didn't have a precise blueprint for achieving this. I believe that Marx had in mind a blurring of work and home, of public and personal life, so that we would no longer distinguish categorically, as Kant did, between the realms of necessity (odious work) and freedom (play). Marx's early vision was the collapsing of work and play, a vision that makes considerable sense when we rethink the boundary between work and home, but only in the direction of humanizing and familizing work, not subjecting the home and personal life to the alienation of labor.

What is alienating about labor? Marx felt that labor in capitalism is alienating because workers don't own the factories and offices and because they don't control their working conditions and the working process. The problem with telework today is that it imports alienated labor—neither owned nor controlled by workers—into the family, boundaried as distinct from the harsh public world of work and politics (see Ehrenreich 1983; Lasch 1977). Marx said that work would only be disalienated under socialism and then communism. But he was vague about how to get there from here. Perhaps a postmodern blurring of work and family, but in the direction of familizing and humanizing work, could initiate this process, with work acquiring elements of play, care, nurturance, and love and home losing its privatized, cut-off quality.

This is very much the agenda of socialist feminism and Freudian Marxism. Marcuse in *Eros and Civilization* (1955) wanted to "erotize" work, to subject it to the rationality of gratification, not the rationality of performance. He felt that this was entirely consistent with an industrial civilization as long as we eliminate what he termed "surplus repression," self-repression beyond the bare minimum necessary for survival and civilization. Pilots and surgeons can still repress their impulses enough that they can do their jobs, but in a socialist/Marcusean society we wouldn't fear that their expertise and self-repression would thwart the rest of us. Most of the rest of us would do erotized, desublimated work that would acquire elements of play and of care, precisely what early Marx had in mind when he sketched his postcapitalist society of praxis. This utopia could be initiated by a familization and humanization of work, but it is stymied by telework conceived as the invasion of home and self by workplace imperatives of productivity and obedience.

The issue is not where you work but how your work affects your life and family, and vice versa. Patterns of time use reveal that we are working harder and longer than ever, diminishing our satisfaction and taking away from family. This is especially injurious to children. Alienated work sets the agenda; we organize family and personal life around it. Time and its compression convert into unhealthy lifestyles: Always in a rush, we eat junk food—aptly named fast food—that clogs our arteries, make us fat, and diminishes our energy. We then engage in fitness routines that cost money and time, purchase gym memberships, follow diets, and consume diet foods. All of this costs money and time. If we lived healthy and nonalienated lives in the first place—lives that are erotized, to use Marcuse's term, based on the familization and humanization of the workplace—none of this would be necessary.

When I talk about the familization and humanization of work I would transform the workplace as much as the family, breaking down distinctions between work time and personal/ family time. We would play at work and work at home. Our work would become play, which is what early Marx and Marcuse had in mind. That seems like an incredible image because we have become accustomed to bureaucratic capitalism in which work is both subdivided and hierarchically coordinated. And home is the patriarchal family that anchors a Protestant capitalism in which parents raise thrifty children, take them to church, and fly the flag on Memorial Day. We cannot reduce alienation in one realm while leaving it intact in another, a key insight of feminists who notice that the personal is political (and the political is personal). Implanting family care and personal meaning in the workplace changes the workplace and also changes the family, inserting it back into the public sphere as an economic and existential unit.

This links class and gender, as left-wing feminists have urged since the late 1960s and early 1970s. Perhaps the most radical demand of the feminist left (indeed of the entire left) was "wages for housework," a recommendation by Mariarosa dalla Costa and Selma James (1973), who keenly understood that capitalist work and the male-dominated family are interlocking. Women do domestic labor for free in order to produce children and reproduce male workers, who perform wage labor. The rhetorical demand for wages for housework sought to valorize (place value on) women's secret labor as cooks, cleaners, child care providers, and sexual partners. It made the strong point that we cannot analytically or politically separate work and home because economic value is produced in both realms.

This discussion demonstrates how we cannot consider work and family, or class and gender, separately. The family is a site of production but not of commodities. What is produced are genders, husbands, meals, children, homework, sex, vacations, yard work, selves. These things are produced in the workplace, too, alongside commodities and services. In a faster capitalism, the boundary between work and family is further broken down as work imperatives colonize the family, children, and selves. But if family and humanity began to colonize work, things would be different, especially if these changes were initiated by women, who think more clearly than men about the hidden factory of gender and family and who have more to gain than men by decolonizing the family and familizing work.

What should the feminist agenda be? Christopher Lasch, a historian sympathetic to the Frankfurt School, argued that we should view the family as a haven in a heartless world (1977). Social policy and activism should defend the family against unwanted intrusions, such as telework. But left-wing feminists such as dalla Costa and James would argue that the family is not, and has never been, a world apart; it is a power structure and work site traditionally run by men (see Eisenstein 1979). Instead of arguing for more rigid boundaries between work and family, these feminists argue for the colonization of work by family and humanity, not only putting day care centers in offices and factories but implanting nurturance, care, love, and opposition to exploitation and violence.

A feminist/Frankfurt School framework for understanding telework, then, emphasizes that such work is usually done by women; that women are still dominated by men in the household; that domestic labor and child care produce unacknowledged and uncompensated economic value; and that the family should be decolonized and should in turn colonize the workplace, setting a pro-family, pro-women, pro-children, pro-worker agenda for the transformation of the workplace (see Walby 1990). Crucial here is that such changes would transform both work and family, leaving neither untouched. Indeed, the ways we think about what is "work" and what is "family" and "private life" would change fundamentally. They are changing anyway, as we allow and encourage people to "office" at home and at Starbucks.

Lengthening the Working Day

Work is omnipresent in faster capitalism now that people can do it anywhere, anytime because of information and communication technologies such as the Internet and laptop computers. The Internet has become a business tool, a literal and figurative network for doing and coordinating work.

It is also very efficient for preparing term papers, planning vacations, e-mailing colleagues, setting up meetings, checking sports scores, and learning about health care. I am a big fan of technology, especially information technology, as long as it does not pollute the environment, contribute to capitalism, or waste our time! After I drop off my kids at school today, I will check my e-mail at a local café before I play tennis. At work later, I will probably check it again and continue work on this book. I will write a review of an article that was sent to me. I will consult Yahoo for the latest news about the war in Iraq. My wife and I may plan our summer vacation using the Internet. This book is not a jeremiad against the Internet and other technologies. It is a consideration of how the Internet accelerates life in capitalism to such an extent that we become appendages of our computers and of capital, and not the other way around. In particular, our time is soaked up as we surf and work, work and surf.

According to postindustrial society theory, people's time use would change as industrial-age progress unfolds. Work would come to occupy a smaller portion of our waking hours as we hand off economic production to technologies. This is already happening, especially in the automotive industry. Marx favored this, too, as he speculated about a good society characterized by "zero work." But he didn't mean that people literally wouldn't work, because, as he explained in his early writings, work is a medium of creativity and identity. What would be reduced to zero, or nearly so, are odious tasks, such as coal mining, that can't be readily humanized and familized. People would do the more creative jobs combining productivity and creativity.

Postindustrial society theory, first authored by Daniel Bell, has been revived by celebrants of the Internet such as Nicholas Negroponte (1996). They argue, among other things, that the Internet and other information technologies will liberate people's time, making them more productive and thus allowing them to work fewer hours. There is no denying that personal computers make old-fashioned typing and office work things of the past. You fire up your computer, write a memo or essay, revise it on the screen, and print it out. With a few keystrokes, you can send it to friends for comment. Inserting graphics is easy, too. And you can do several things at once, using "windows" that you open and close as you need them. You can write your paper, listen to music, read and write e-mail messages, and look up things on the Web, with few transaction costs. This is bound to make people more productive.

But has all of this diminished work? Studies of time use suggest otherwise. Workers may be more productive, but this is less because they use these new technologies than because they log more hours behind the desk or on the road using a laptop. When domestic technologies such as vacuum cleaners were first introduced, for women primarily, they were advertised as "labor-saving." But they have actually created a need for work, cluttering people's lives with chores that they didn't previously do (see Cowan 1985). The Internet is exactly the same as the vacuum cleaner: Because it is there, we use it. And, unlike the vacuum cleaner, it possesses "connectivity"; it follows us everywhere, compelling us to use it at work, at home, anywhere. Now we can even check and compose e-mail messages using our cell phones.

Why are people working more? There is no single reason. People are working more than their forebears in the 1950s because the economy requires two-earner families and additional marginal hours of work in order to pay the bills, especially credit card debt; they work more because information technologies tempt them not to leave the job at the office but to take it home; they work more because work has become a sheltered harbor in which people are relieved of the stresses of home, family, and parenting. Work is leisure, and leisure work. People want to avoid the stress of family and kids, and work connects them to others, affording them adult community, both face-to-face and virtual. This is especially true for women who shoulder the housework and child care responsibilities but at work enjoy a measure of equality with male colleagues. Finally, and perhaps most important, our capitalist economy colonizes private life, personal time, because it wants people to be productive and not distracted. Capitalism wants people to be "on task," for which the Internet, e-mail, cell phones, fax machines, and pagers are perfectly suited.

Your boss can chase you down at home and on the weekend. He can give you assignments and monitor your performance. I was once an academic administrator, which, in the university world, is almost like having a real job, with 9–5 accountability. Actually, it is somewhat like being a corporate executive in that you are expected to be at work earlier than 9 a.m. and to leave later than 5 p.m., and also to work weekends. I had a "boss" who called me at home at exactly 8 a.m. on a weekday to summon me to his office. The implicit message was that I should have been at work. He told me that he wanted my middle managers at their desks by 9 a.m., when he could call them. Contradictorily, this particular boss was not an Internet person, and didn't do e-mail. Grudgingly, he realized that "everyone else" used it, and so he delegated the task of receiving and answering his e-mail to his secretary. He would compose his responses in longhand, not caring that this was inefficient. He didn't fully comprehend that e-mail could fill people's time and keep them accountable, and I resented his old-fashioned expectation that I must be in my office in order to do my job.

Actually, my boss's "old-fashioned" values were only as old as a decade ago, before people worked virtually anytime, anywhere. This is a mixed picture: In the bad old days of

Weber's bureaucracy and Taylor's time-and-motion studies, authority and accountability were harsh (see Bendix 1956). Workers were tied to their machines and their offices, the workday and workweek were rigid, and time was inflexible. Today, in the wired world of our faster capitalism, time oozes everywhere, possessing great elasticity. You can meet your boss's expectations from your office desk, your home office, the local coffee shop, on a plane using a laptop—or even from the beach. This is less harsh than Taylor's regime and even the corporate culture of the 1950s, from which my former boss hailed. In effect, a virtual capitalism has decoupled time and space—the time it takes to perform a task and the physical space in which that is accomplished. It doesn't matter "where" you work, given telecommuting, teleconferencing, e-mail, faxes, cell phones, and courier services.

You can be nocturnal if that is your preference, or awaken at 6 a.m., the way I do. My best writing hour is between 6 and 7 a.m., after which I help get my kids ready for school and then drive them there. I play tennis or lift weights after that; after showering, I'm in my office by eleven. I answer e-mail and do some more writing, after which I knock off for lunch. In the afternoon, I read, fish, watch sports or the news. In the witching hour before dinner, from 5 to 6 p.m., I may do some more writing, reenergized by my day and having allowed the morning's writing to simmer and stew. I may spend no more than two or three hours a day writing, although I'm always thinking about the book I'm writing (and perhaps the one after that). In these intense two or three hours of writing, I may compose five pages or, if I'm on a roll, as many as ten. I get a lot written, using my desktop computers or laptop, but I don't spend many tortured hours doing it. I want and need a life, recognizing, after twenty-five years of academic writing, that my literary energies are best spent when I'm really fresh and have something to say. If I write when I am tired, unfocused, preoccupied, or diverted, it's a waste of time. On such issues of time and academic writing, see Zerubavel (1999), who plans his writing schedule more meticulously than I do; it works for him.

This is the intellectual life as I live it. Accountability freaks who operate with "old-fashioned," pre-Internet, pre–information technology mind-sets may disdain this time use as loafing. But I'm a tenured professor, and tenured professors don't face many constraints. It may be the only nonalienated job in America. Academia finds us because we are nonlinear, noncorporate, nonconformist. The vast majority of workers today don't enjoy tenure or its equivalent. For them, information technologies aren't necessarily a convenience, let alone a salvation. They are electronic prostheses that tether workers to the job site and to productivity expectations. Indeed, my thesis is that people's lives and their time are becoming more cluttered with work as they "office" elsewhere than in their traditional cubicles. This is a paradox: the less time people spend in traditional workspaces and -places, the more they work both because *they can* and because *it is expected of them*. The Internet is both tether and noose, positioning people to be accountable, to work all the time, and to neglect their personal lives, selves, and families.

One risks technological determinism in these claims. I am not isolating the Internet, cell phones, and pagers as the sole means of deepening domination. People work because capitalism needs them to contribute to production and to match this production with shopping, which can also be done electronically. Capitalism has always attempted to maximize productivity; now, fast work both intensifies and lengthens the workday. Capitalism also wants to divert people from their own alienation, especially as overall wealth is sufficient to liberate people the world over from desperate poverty. Finally, as capitalism lurches from boom to bust and back again, people need marginal dollars as their real incomes fall, especially if they separate and divorce. These extra dollars are derived from extra hours worked, which are made possible by the electronic prostheses linking private life to production.

A SERVICE ECONOMY?

The centerpiece of postindustrial society was to be the substitution of clean, white-collar work for dirty and dangerous blue-collar work. This has begun to occur in advanced capitalist economies. However, we need to examine the segmentation of the labor force and occupations before we embrace this prophecy. There is not simply a single "white-collar work," benign and well compensated, but different types of such work, all of which could be said to provide services. Doctors, lawyers, social workers, psychiatrists, professors, teachers, artists, advertisers, corporate executives: all of these workers are relatively well compensated and creative. But let's lengthen the list: fast-food workers, retail sales clerks, office clerical workers, waitresses. These service jobs involve low skill levels and low pay; they are rarely unionized; if they work fewer than thirty hours a week, these workers are not provided with benefits.

Barbara Ehrenreich, in her rich ethnography of dead-end work in America, *Nickel and Dimed* (2001), performed such jobs, concealing the fact that she is a left-wing intellectual. Her portrayal of this kind of work is thoroughly dismal. In the past ten years, job creation in the U.S. economy has occurred mainly in these low-end, minimum-wage service jobs, for which only meager literacy is required. The segmentation of the labor force describes the bifurcation of good and bad jobs, those that require skill, training, and education (and are rewarded with good pay, benefits, and a career ladder) and those that don't (and are rewarded with low pay, few or no benefits, and no career ladder). Sometimes, sociologists distinguish between *careers* and *jobs*. Careers are typically white collar and professional, while jobs are blue collar and manual. But in an informatic faster capitalism we see a new occupational category, called by Coupland (1991) "McJobs," referring to their fast-food-franchise-like nature, including minimum-wage pay.

73

Economists and politicians who want to brag about job creation sometimes mislabel these McJobs as real jobs, even as white-collar careers, because they are located in the supposedly clean service sector of the economy. But there are obvious differences between having your taxes prepared by a professional accountant (a service) and having your carpets cleaned by temporary workers or your dog walked by a college student (also services). A faster capitalism proliferates these service-sector McJobs because people in a bind for time increasingly rely on service providers such as fast-food restaurants, maid services, and gardeners to meet their needs. As time compresses and accelerates, people need services performed for them, all the way from buying take-out meals to having one's windows cleaned.

This service work cannot be readily disentangled from other changes in the economy and family, such as dual-career families, the acceleration of childhood, lengthy commutes and carpooling, and people's loss of skill when it comes to self-care. Americans eat out frequently, indirectly creating jobs for cooks and servers. They eat out because they don't have time to cook and their cooking skills have declined. Restaurant food tends to be fattening, so consumers join gyms for exercise. When they visit the gym, they either leave their kids with a babysitter or take them to the gym's day care facility. What I just described creates many new jobs, but it makes people more dependent on service providers. They are less self-sufficient and self-regulating in a service-oriented economy.

What are cause and effect here? Do patterns of consumption drive job creation? Or do patterns of consumption follow from changes in the economy and the ways that people's working lives affect their personal and family lives? Although Marx assigned economic factors primacy, he was careful to point out the inseparability of work and family, of production and consumption. I choose to emphasize what I am calling *acceleration,* the speeding up of work and family that compresses time so that people have too little of it, leading them

74

to consume services and thus creating service-sector jobs. These service jobs aren't the white-collar careers glorified by apologists such as Daniel Bell but dead-end, stupefying McJobs of the kind described by Ehrenreich. The working poor now wear the aprons of cleaning services and Wal-Mart bibs instead of the overalls of yesteryear. More have McJobs than even a decade ago because people's lives are so accelerated that they don't have time to cook, clean, babysit, or mow their lawns.

We pay several prices for this acceleration: The poor souls who work at Wal-Mart and McDonald's almost by definition can't make ends meet; they endure a cycle of poverty, despair, and anxiety described by Ehrenreich. People who always eat out and rely on maids lose self-reliance, shared family time, and healthful lifestyles. Their work is omnipresent, shrinking their personal and family time and its quality. By shifting work away from industrial production and toward the provision of services, we may sustain the illusion of postindustrial progress instead of recognizing labor-market segmentation as a perennial manifestation of class structure, as Marx identified it. Finally, by assigning McJobs predominantly to young people, we short-circuit their educations and don't challenge them intellectually. As Schlosser notes in *Fast Food Nation* (2001), the dream of the fast-food industry is kitchen technology so obvious that one needs virtually no training or literacy to operate the ovens, grills, and dishwashing machines. Zero work, the mantra of postindustrialists, has been replaced by zero training as the goal of service-sector managers.

Stratification by age isn't the only feature of labor-market segmentation, split between careers and McJobs. There is also ample stratification by race and ethnicity, as the working poor are mainly black and Hispanic. This compounds class inequalities, blending them with inequalities of race and ethnicity that promote discrimination, hate crime, low self-esteem, and the cycle of urban poverty. White people, especially in cities and in the South, become accustomed to being serviced by non-whites, sending powerful messages to children on both sides of the class/race divide. Gender, too, is part of this portrait: Ehrenreich describes jobs done mainly by women, such as housecleaning and waitressing. Postindustrial society theory suggested that poverty would be eliminated as the underclasses worked their way out of the station of their birth by acquiring education, literacy, and skills. Instead, in a faster capitalism, structures of class, race, and gender inequality are becoming further entrenched.

MUST WORK EXPAND?

I began this chapter by noticing that the working day has become longer, not shorter, as people work more and harder in multiple sites and with flexible technologies binding them to the job. This has eroded private life and families. Work has expanded both because capitalism is a sweatshop in its basic imperative of ever-increasing profit, which requires ever-increasing work and ever-increasing consumption, and because it *can* expand, given technologies of virtuality. Information technologies are almost a demiurge, possessing a life and will of their own, replacing themselves with newer, more invasive, more accelerated versions every few years, whether there is a real need for them or not. Take televisions. When I was a kid, we watched a basic old black-and-white TV. There was no cable, only a funky antenna that we had to jiggle to get decent reception. Shows began at 6 or 7 a.m., and they were over by midnight, if not earlier. Cartoons were broadcast on Saturday mornings and perhaps for an hour after school. In Eugene, Oregon, where I grew up, we received the three major networks and, later, a public-broadcasting station. We had one TV set for as long as I can remember.

Then came color. I remember watching color television for the first time when I was in my twenties. It was a professional football game, and the players had surreal green outlines. The field looked blueish. I noticed then that people were purchasing multiple television sets, deployed in bedrooms, living rooms, even kitchens. By the time I was in my thirties, televisions were being miniaturized. At the turn of the twenty-first century, we have moved to DVD and plasma technologies and flat, thin screens with decorator designs. My family and I were in Best Buy recently and we noticed state-of-the-art televisions retailing for $12,000. We paid a couple of hundred bucks for our basic color model with a 16-inch screen.

Televisions entertain and divert. They are also profitable commodities for an industry that, truth be told, could have stopped at basic color. HDTV barely improves the quality of the picture, and, even if it did, who needs to spend thousands of dollars for a television, especially when many middle-class households have several? Although television is watched in leisure time, people have to work extra hours in order to pay for their expensive rigs. Television is a false need that leads to additional work. Take another postmodern technology, the cell phone. Many people above the poverty line seem to have them, and even some below. You pay $50 or more a month for the privilege. Although they, too, are entertaining and afford people connection in an anonymous, fast-moving world, they are a working tool, allowing one to stay in touch with the office and colleagues and bosses to stay in touch with you. Cell phones are the cost, and the medium, of doing business today for most people in sales and services.

Cell phones, like other technological innovations that both accelerate time and compress space, are a dialectical phenomenon: They have positive and negative features, and their ultimate social impact is as yet unclear, given the coexistence of these positives and negatives. Such dialectical phenomena must be acted on by people in order to determine whether they are ultimately progressive or regressive. Cells allow people to connect with each other with much more flexibility than is afforded by land lines. In a mobile society, this allows people to maintain and create social relationships over time and space. This is crucial as people, especially women, negotiate the boundary between work and family; you can talk on your cell phone while you drive to pick up your kids or while you sit in the bleachers at their softball practice. But the price of connection, for both community and convenience, is the long arm of the office. There is no downtime for people who have cells. They are always accessible and available.

Michel Foucault (1977) wrote about "discipline" as a new condition of domination. Discipline, he emphasizes, is both imposed and self-imposed; people do it "to" themselves as well as have it done to them. Understanding the duality of discipline is crucial to understanding the omnipresence of work, especially as people use new information technologies such as cell phones and computers in order to work longer hours and allow their homes and selves to be overtaken by production imperatives. There is a psychology and social psychology of feeling accountable, of wanting to be accountable. Turning your cell phone off or lacking daily or even hourly access to e-mail causes anxiety for people who want to be plugged in and don't want to miss anything in the workplace. This is because they have been trained to be productive and accountable and don't want to be left behind. It is no longer enough, and perhaps never was, to do one's job. One needs to go beyond the call of duty, not extraordinarily but routinely as work hours expand to 24/7. This is both done "to" workers, who resent their bosses' and colleagues' intrusions at home, and "by" workers, who become addicted to instantaneity, which is the lived experience of a faster capitalism.

The ubiquity of cell phones, e-mail, and pagers (which are now almost obsolete) blurs the boundaries between work and family. One uses the cell phone and e-mail to facilitate both work relationships and personal and family relationships. One can use call interrupt to "multitask," which is an interesting way to deal with compressed time and multiple demands that cut across the public/private boundary. Who hasn't had the experience of talking to one's child or a friend on the phone when a call from the workplace beeps through? You can put your personal life on hold, literally, while dealing with the office query, and then slide back into personal mode, using anytime/anywhere minutes. Time is literally money as cell-phone providers charge by the minute, with variable rates for evenings and weekends. These charges are viewed as necessary, fixed costs, much as people treat cable television and high-speed Internet connections as basic services without which one cannot conduct contemporary work and family life.

REDEFINING SOCIAL INSTITUTIONS TEMPORALLY

This discussion of work's expansion suggests new sociological concepts with which to describe social structures and social institutions. Institutions are no longer simply a configuration of typical activities that meet supposed social purposes, such as the economy or media. They are patterns of time use. Work is how much time you spend during an average week or month in the office, on the road, on the phone, on the computer, worrying, hoping, networking, strategizing. It is also the hidden time spent cleaning clothes, making meals, getting ready in the morning, restoring oneself physically and spiritually. Family is how much time you spend on kids, your spouse or partner, yourself. There is overlap when, for example, you host a Christmas party to which colleagues and neighbors are invited, when you attend your child's soccer game and network with other parents who could become business contacts, or when you work out with colleagues at the company gym. I am defining institutions as the time we spend on activities and not on place- or space-driven activities (such as time spent in the physical office or in the physical home) because, with information and communications technologies, we can work at home and do personal things at work, such as surfing, chatting, phoning, and e-mailing.

Work, then, is not simply the physical place in which we do it, nor our job titles, nor our intellectual and physical motion. It is the time we spend doing it, which disconnects it from space and place. Frederick Taylor, the author of an approach to maximizing (Marx would say exploiting) labor by examining its time and motion (1967), placed heavy emphasis on the duration of tasks. But he assumed that work, mainly physical in nature, would occur in fixed sites such as factories and along assembly lines pioneered by his contemporary Henry Ford. But in a faster capitalism, work's pace is quickened because it can be done anywhere, anytime. At issue, then, in redefining work as an institution temporally is noticing that work can be done anywhere and that this affects work's identity as a separable, singular activity that can be put aside when one enters another social institution such as family, leisure, or education.

Work's omnipresence lies in its anywhere/anytime-ness (using e-mail and cell phones) and in its encroachment into other domains no longer temporally separable from it. If you can "work" at "home," then the definition of home as a separate social institution changes. Although work can be humanized and familized, as I indicated earlier, the colonization of one institution by another tends to be a one-way flow in fast capitalism: Although we can put our kids in workplace day care facilities, the personalization, familization, humanization, and erotization of work, driven by personal and family imperatives that Freud and Marcuse call Eros or the life instincts, are blunted by capitalism. In other words, capitalist managers resist the tendency of family to flow into work, fearing that work would be disalienated and democratized, thus changing its very nature and the very nature of the capitalist economic system. Work may invade family, temporally, but family cannot invade work beyond the extent to which workers care for their kids, either on-site or remotely.

This is not a perfect plan; people resist and react creatively. There are only so many hours in the day and thus people cannot work all the time, although they often seem to. Workers, especially women, use the telephone and Internet to plan for their children's care during the day, after school, and in the summer. It is remarkable that the United States doesn't have a national child care policy or, as has often been lamented, a national health care policy. It is simply assumed by employers and by the state that workers will use their private ingenuity to take care of their children, even though school ends at around 3 p.m. and summer begins by late May or mid-June. My wife and I have little trouble in juggling our schedules and our work to accommodate our kids' school day or their summer schedule. But even our untenured colleagues, especially those who commute over significant distances, cannot afford to be so laconic. They feel pressured, as do all private-sector workers in America, to occupy their physical cubicles and to network up and down the corridor.

People with "real," 9–5 jobs are confronted by the long reach of productivity expectations when they are "off" work, which further erodes their time and autonomy. In addition, they must find a way to be parents, spouses, partners, and selves. As time compresses in faster capitalism, they resist the speedup of work and life by spending ostensible work time on other things, especially children and family. Sneak a peak at any office worker's computer screen and chances are you will find people busily surfing the Internet and e-mailing on topics that have nothing to do with the job at hand. Listen in on their phone conversations and chances are you will hear people planning and coordinating their complex lives, juggling pediatric appointments for the kids, volunteer work at their schools, a lunch among friends, getting a new roof, and dealing with the insurance company. There are two notable trends here: People are spending more time working both because they can and because they are expected to do so. Also, the decompartmentalization of institutions, with work bleeding into family and vice versa, occasions a redistribution of time so that we now "do" family and personal life at work and work at home, even if we do more total work.

People resist the speedup and they resent work's colonization of self and family. They juggle because they have to. Beneficent bosses understand this and realize that being flexible is a surer route to overall productivity than is cracking the whip. They realize that an afternoon off for one of their employees is time well spent because gratitude begets productivity. Not all managers see it this way, especially male ones. In this case, employees resent their insensitivity and resist what amounts to a speedup. When called in for work on a weekend, they may suddenly have to visit an ailing aunt. Women with children look for jobs and bosses who cut them slack. They look for bosses who are women or men with children and who empathize. This leads to the concerns of my following chapter, where I consider the impact of accelerated life on family and childhood. It is already clear from this chapter that a deboundarying of work and home makes it difficult to sustain the illusion that the family is a haven in a heartless world. But there is a dialectical twist here, as always: Family, as we have begun to see in this chapter, provides a utopian model for reorganizing work—what I have called familization.

4

Fast Families and Virtual Children

Fast capitalism fades the boundaries between institutions; postmodern theorists call this dedifferentiation. Of particular interest is the boundary between home and work or school. In this chapter, I discuss the impact of acceleration on families and on their virtual children. Since the end of the 1980s, but beginning long before that, we have gradually removed the boundaries around the family that protect people within it, especially children. This is partly because the family has become a work site and a shopping mall. We have also turned schools into workplaces. Everyone works harder and harder, in official workplaces, in the home, and in schools, which are increasingly organized along workplace principles. The casualties of all this are time, and, in particular, childhood, a particularly important time.

FAST FAMILIES

I have discussed the ways in which people take their jobs home with them. Information technologies such as the Internet, cell phones, personal computers, laptops, fax machines, and pagers make this possible. People work longer hours because they can, they are always available to their bosses and colleagues, and they internalize the expectation of hard work. They also work longer hours because they need to pay off credit cards on which they have billed all sorts of commodities and services, regarded as luxuries by the standards of earlier generations.

During the Middle Ages and before, families and households were routinely regarded as places of work, especially agriculture (see Shorter 1975). The work/family distinction didn't crystallize until as late as the Victorian era in nineteenth-century English capitalism. The Victorians persuaded women to remove themselves, and their children, from factories so that they wouldn't compete with men for jobs. The family was idealized as a retreat for men after a hard working day. Women were valued as caregivers, helpmates, chefs, cleaners, and mothers, roles for which the Victorians and Freud found them ideally suited, given their alleged intuition and maternal empathy.

Women remained at home from the end of the nineteenth century until just after halfway through the twentieth. With the women's movement in the 1960s, women were given full citizenship both as political actors and as economic agents. They went to work alongside men, although, curiously, they remain primarily responsible for the household and children. As I noted in chapter 3, women are increasingly pressed for time, doing both paid work and domestic work. Families and households today are more likely to have two earners than one, a fateful outcome of the admixture of Victorianism and feminism.

By the beginning of the twenty-first century, the household has been transformed from what it was when I grew up in the tranquil late 1950s and early 1960s. My mom stayed at home; we didn't eat out every night. Occasionally, we went to the movies, but never to the mall, which didn't yet exist in Eugene, Oregon. Today, families and households are frenzied sites of multiple roles, obligations, lifestyles, diets, exercise regimes, computing, phoning, television, movies, and music. The fast family has become a pit stop along the information superhighway. It is the site of homework, take-out meals, nighttime entertainment, and sleep (what little there is of it).

To portray the slower family, that of my childhood, as a golden age is an exaggeration and ignores the plight of women assigned chores and caretaking but not given income or political purchase. Betty Friedan in her *Feminine Mystique* (1963) started second-wave American feminism (the first wave was the fight for suffrage, the right to vote) by noticing that suburban moms, like my own, were bored to death using labor-saving devices such as vacuum cleaners, toasters, washing machines, and dryers. After their kids went to school in the morning, they could be done with housework by noon. Their main challenge was to fill time with the manufactured busyness of bridge clubs and tennis lessons. For middle-class women who don't work, filling time and the void of meaning are still their main challenges. As Friedan emphasized, staying home, when most others go to work, can be stultifying and lonely. By the same token, though, work is alienating and stressful for most workers, both men and women. It seems that neither men nor women are getting their needs met.

The fast family is also unfair to women, saddling them with stressful jobs and a higher incidence of stress-related illnesses such as heart disease and strokes, while still requiring them to prepare meals, clean the house, and help the kids with homework. Although fast capitalism liberates women to work alongside men, and even as their bosses, it stresses them out by depriving them of time, which is even scarcer for them than it is for men, at least those men who don't pitch in around the house and with the kids (see Blumstein and Schwartz 1983). Friedan's 1950s suburban white women had too much time; today's women, liberated by Friedan's book and the women's movement it helped initiate, have too little, and their families are necessarily changing as a result.

The fast family doesn't commune. There is little "connection." Meals are eaten out or brought in. There is little dialogue or discussion. Children learn to talk and think by listening to their parents and by engaging with them verbally. The fast family is noisy and busy, but it is less verbal than families were before. Family members are monads: they plug in to their MP3 players; they watch television or videos on their own TV sets in their own rooms; they use computers to surf and chat in isolation. They even eat separately and on the run. Parents chauffeur kids to sports and lessons, dropping them off until the time is up or sitting in their cars talking on their cells. Neglect and anomie prevail.

Fatigue is chronic. Nearly a majority of Americans complain about not getting enough sleep. Parents and kids stay up too late, plugged in to technologies that entertain and numb. Kids have collegelike amounts homework, which they must delay until after their sports practices and games are over. I know eight-, nine-, ten-, and eleven-year-olds who have weekday baseball and soccer games that don't start until 8 p.m. or later. They are, in effect, on adult schedules, even though they have a much greater need for sleep than do adults. They are becoming like adults, who create children in their own images.

As family connection and community decline, culture and work intrude. It is difficult to disentangle cause and effect. Single-cause theories—television is ruining civilization!—are tempting but should be resisted. As the world beats down the door, people develop identities inimical to communing. They become privatized, alone unto themselves. The virtual self is too frequently nonverbal, staring at the screen and perhaps interacting with distant, anonymous others using their screen names. My daughter's classmates are babysat after school by AOL's free chat rooms in which they gather to mingle with each other. In Eugene, in the early 1960s, I gathered after school with my friends to play in the park down the street. We had nicknames, not screen names. We walked home together, and sometimes my friends would stay for dinner. My parents knew these many itinerants well, their favorite foods, their addresses, their parents and their occupations, even their nicknames. We were part of a neighborhood extended family, grounded in home and school seamlessly connected.

We were much less worldly than kids and their parents today. My daughter's classmates know about sex, cars, celebrities, and professional sports. In seventh grade, I knew very little about culture and the world, even though my father was a liberal professor. In retrospect, it is clear that he and my mother shielded me and my sister from the world, even though I was offered careful lessons about political and racial justice, given my dad's values. Although I knew what my dad did for a living (he frequently took me to his university office) and he sometimes worked at home, the time he spent at home was largely devoted to the family. We went on vacations together, usually by car. We owned a small cabin without electricity, where we would spend idyllic summers fishing and doing things outdoors. These are indelible memories. Electronic culture plays virtually no role in any of this, apart from evenings before bed spent listening, on my parents' shortwave radio, to San Francisco Giants and San Francisco Warriors games for a few minutes before lights out.

We went to Europe when I was thirteen, and things changed. My eyes were opened to a world beyond Eugene, Roosevelt Junior High, the Oregon Ducks, and trout fishing on the McKenzie River. I discovered England, the Netherlands, Italy, France, Germany, Yugoslavia, Poland, Czechoslovakia, the Soviet Union. I was exposed to their music, their newspapers, their intellectual work. I returned to Europe to study during the summers of my college years, drinking deeply of social philosophy and critical theory. These odysseys changed my life, all for the better. I was no longer parochial, and I came to hate small-town life, middle America, malls, materialism. But cosmopolitanism, in my case, came gently, all in good time, through slow boats, slow walks through foreign cities, slow dinners under starlit European nights. It was built on a stable base of family, community, and identity.

My wife and I took our kids to Paris a few years ago. We stayed a week, just long enough for us to recover from jet lag. My daughter loved the foreignness of the place, its incredible architecture, the accents, the food, EuroDisney. I suspect that this short visit changed her, and possibly even my younger son, in ways that will make sense to her only when she looks back from the distant vantage of maturity. In the meantime, since September 11 and the war in Iraq, the world has become too dangerous for family travel by air to Europe. Our kids learned of the events of September 11 at school, even before we had an opportunity to talk to them. They watched replays of the towers collapsing, of the war in Afghanistan, and now the war in Iraq. We shield them when we can, but they talk of such events in social studies class, which is not a bad thing. After all, we talked of the Kennedy assassinations, the war in Vietnam, and civil rights. Unlike their classmates, they don't wear patriotic clothing. But kids today are disenchanted, inured to screen violence, inhumanity, bestial crimes, wars. My daughter glanced at television one night when four-thousand-pound bombs, "bunker busters," were dropped on Saddam Hussein's hiding place, perhaps killing his two sons. No matter Hussein's misdeeds, this has a heartbreaking, poignant quality to it—the live broadcast of probable death and its interrogation by CNN pundits (see Kellner 2003).

Families are inundated by such images, which flow through coaxial cables, DSL lines, and satellite dishes. Families rent explicit movies, and while watching television during family hour they hear talk of sex and scatology. We were watching an episode of a popular and relatively elevated family-hour drama another night, and the perky protagonist, a woman in her thirties named Carol, said "son of a bitch." My kids heard that and were nonplussed: These are not words we want them to hear. And yet cultural sanction was being provided for them by network television. It is not enough simply to turn off television or not own one in the first place. Other kids watch television, and their worldliness is displayed at the lunch table and in the halls between classes. My daughter learned about prostitutes from fifth-grade boys who not only watch adult television and movies but also surf the Web un-constrained by parental restrictions on content. This robs her of innocence and forces her to grow up too quickly. She's not yet an adolescent and she has been exposed, by her peers (and they by their parents and culture), to worldly influences for which she is unprepared. Although my wife and I are progressive, talk openly about everything, and can undo some of these influences, my daughter is caught up in the acceler-ation of family, culture, and childhood in spite of herself and in spite of our best efforts to insulate her.

Fast families are fast temporally, in terms of adults' and kids' hurried routines, especially where paid work and home-work invade previously inviolable "off" hours (see Hochschild 1989). They are also fast in terms of their exposure to the world—advertising, entertainment, adult themes. It is difficult not to be cynical, and to grow up cynical, in a culture of "reality," as certain cinema verité television shows are now called. "Reality" invades and intrudes, conducted by informa-tion and entertainment technologies that break down barriers between social institutions characteristic of earlier stages of modernity. Virtual selves are formed, and form themselves, from the flotsam and jetsam of culture, news, "reality," to which they have instant access. In this context, it is difficult for family to nurture children, allowing them to grow up in a protected environment unsullied by "reality."

THE ACCELERATION AND ABOLITION OF CHILDHOOD

Before the Industrial Revolution and subsequent Victorianism, which convinced women to withdraw from the workforce into the family, the category of *the child* did not exist, as Edward Shorter explains in *The Making of the Modern Family* (1975). Children were miniature adults expected to work alongside their parents in agricultural communities. Childhood was not viewed as a precious, vulnerable time, nor as a developmental sequence leading to adulthood. Once the child could walk and talk, he was expected to shoulder adult responsibilities. In preindustrial countries and cultures today, this is still the rule: Families are large so that there is an ample domestic work supply, especially where infant mortality robs families of helping hands.

In England, as industrial capitalism matured, laws against child labor were enacted in order to acknowledge the developmental needs of six- and seven-year-olds. The Victorian era, which saw women's retreat from paid labor in order to tend children and the household, redefined childhood as a special time for birthdays, Christmas, and play. Childhood was acknowledged as an important, indeed perhaps the most important, stage of personal development, linking infancy and adulthood. Psychologists and family sociologists developed elaborate theories and empirical literatures exploring this fertile period.

The notion of the precious child has been central to capitalist Victorian-influenced culture for over a century. For those of us who grew up during the late 1950s and 1960s, it would have been unthinkable that childhood could be anything less than a golden age, given the power of a media culture enshrining what we more recently came to call family values. Situation comedies extolled the virtues of family and carefully delineated male and female roles, which feminists later termed the sexual division of labor. Women were portrayed as better suited emotionally and pragmatically to taking care of the kids and household, while men were framed as more suited to the cutthroat world of work, in which they build bridges and engineer corporate mergers.

The idealization of childhood, and its management by mom, was given sociological voice by Talcott Parsons and his conservative structural-functionalist sociological theory. In *The Social System* (1951), he defended the sexual division of labor and the role of children within it on "functional" grounds: It makes more sense for the sexes to do what they do best, women to nurture, care, clean, and men to fabricate, navigate, litigate.

Feminists point out that Parsons was merely reflecting the gender relations and roles of post–World War II America, in which women had once again been convinced to retreat from war-era work performed while the men were out soldiering. Women's retreat to the middle-class suburban home was transformed by Parsons and other gender ideologists from a necessity into a virtue.

Feminists of the 1960s such as Betty Friedan, Gloria Steinem, and Germaine Greer, inspired by Simone de Beauvoir's *The Second Sex* (1953), assailed the sexual division of labor as unfair to women. They understood that Parsons's and *Reader's Digest*'s notions of the boundaried family, humanized by women, concealed economic and political exploitation of women, who were denied access to education, jobs, and political office. A decade later, theorists such as Nancy Chodorow (1978), blending Freud and feminism, took this argument one step further by noticing that the sexual division of labor—indeed, gender roles generally—harms both little boys and little girls. It harms boys where the father is absent from the family and from childrearing. The boy, in order to separate himself from his doting mother, learns to hate women. Little girls don't have useful models of their future relations with men because their dads are so frequently absent, and they resent their mothers, toward whom they have enduring ambivalence. Now the real world isn't as neat, or as deterministic, as all this. But Chodorow is observing that the ways in which we construct gender in the context of family relations is harmful to all parties, including children, where it denies both sexes opportunities for emotions, intimacy, and a paycheck heretofore reserved for only one of the sexes.

In any case, as capitalism has accelerated throughout the twentieth century and into the twenty-first, it is no longer clear that "the child" is even a useful category. This will seem scandalous and excessive to child psychologists, family sociologists, and Republicans, not to mention born-again Christians. Surely children, as biological entities, haven't disappeared. But there has been a stunning—one might even say a postmodern—reversal of the values attached to life stages, here childhood, since Victorians first idealized the cherished cherub as the centerpiece of domestic life. We are, in effect, reverting to premodern conceptions of the child as a small and not particularly needy adult; we have broken down barriers separating family from society in such a way that we have come to expect children to be adults. This is manifested in sexuality, schooling, sports, and what one might loosely call worldliness.

THE GENDERED CHILD

By the time you are reading this, my daughter will have completed her first year of junior high school. Throughout her sixth-grade year, she has regaled my wife and me with stories of preadolescent dating by some of her classmates, mainly the "cool" kids, who are physically developed, perhaps because their birthdays fall earlier in the year. There are other aspects of coolness, including clothing, comportment, and charisma. Frequently, it is enough for kids to anoint themselves cool for the label to take effect as social differentiation occurs—cool kids, geeks, kids somewhere in the middle.

Social differentiation in the preteen and early teen years is primarily about, and for, girls (Dellasega 2001). Eleven- and twelve-year-old girls are more socially developed than their male counterparts, who seem like clods and dunces by comparison. But accompanying girls' social intelligence are interpersonal intrigue and intimidation that lead to bullying and marginalization. For the most part, my daughter's male classmates just play sports and try to ignore the fact that they are on the verge of their teenage years. They must be dragged along to cotillion class and even on "dates" with classmates arranged by their mothers (Hersch 1998).

I vaguely remember liking girls in elementary school. But dating was delayed until high school, and even then it was casual by today's standards. The older, physically developed, middle- and upper-middle-class kids in my daughter's grade not only "date" (I must put the word in quotation marks because it isn't a real date if mommy takes you and attends); they also "go steady." The term today is *going out,* as in "Johnny is going out with Suzie." Going out is, again, a falsehood. At most, these dyads attend the occasional movie and may chat in school. But these pairings and this incipient sexual behavior are *mimicry,* expressions of what the culture tells these kids that adults do. These eleven- and twelve-year-olds watch *Friends* and *Baywatch* reruns; they enter adult chat rooms; they find sex pages on the Web. They have become worldly in ways that include sexuality, although it is a premature sexuality jarringly inconsistent with the media images of adult sexuality to which they are exposed.

This raises important questions about the connection between capitalism and sexuality. The same capitalism that thwarts genuine creativity and connection provokes people to *sexualize* themselves as an alternative. People are creatures of an intense desire (Eros, in Freud's terms) that seeks gratification. This gratification can be enduring, when, for example, a painter paints a masterpiece. Or it can be ephemeral and superficial, for example when a person wins a small amount of money in a lottery or when a person adorns himself or herself for the opposite (or same) sex and is judged "hot." Anonymous sexual release is also an example of ephemeral gratification, although I hasten to add that in a nonalienating society people wouldn't shun sex; indeed, as Marcuse argues, all of their human relationships would be "erotized," that is, subject to what he and Freud call the pleasure principle.

Today, sex is compartmentalized, referring to a slice of life, not all of erotized human relationships, as Marcuse envisaged. It stands at one remove from desire, Eros, the life instinct. Indeed, it often stands at two removes, with pornography on the Internet and in videos and magazines. Voyeurism replaces even compartmentalized sex, contact between two real bodies

F2F, or, perhaps, B2B. Eric Schlosser tells this story well in *Reefer Madness* (2003), where he describes the informal, underground market for sex and drugs, including pornographic videos and Web sites. Huge business is done on the Internet, where people pay money to watch other people have "live" sex. It is "live" only in the sense that it is taking place in real time. It is simulated (not live) in that people are performing for the camera, as they do in pornographic movies. This is not what Marcuse (1955) had in mind when he talked of a sexualized, erotized society in which people could gratify themselves and others by the sheer intimacy, closeness, and care of their relationships, which extend from the bedroom to the workplace.

Sexuality spills over into gender, where a person's biological sexuality blends with his conception of masculinity or her conception of femininity. We construct gender in order to find a secure niche in the prevailing binary structure of genders, either as "masculine" or "feminine." Sexuality, especially on the levels of adornment/appearance and fantasy, is tightly bound with gender identity: A sexy woman is one who has big breasts, painted nails, and revealing clothes. In reproducing gender, we reproduce the sexual division of labor, patriarchy, economic inequality between the sexes, and women's objectification, even violence against women. Feminists oppose the bipolarity of supposedly masculine and feminine traits and urge the sharing of parenting, working, and housework. Gender is a prison.

The sexualized child is constructed by the sexualized adult, who seeks solace in sex isolated from other social institutions and who would reproduce gender identity in children. Sexuality and gender are learned from parents, who have a stake in a certain normalcy, as they understand it. In my daughter's class, many girls are already clearly feminized, that is, they have acquired women's gender identity. Many shave their legs, wear makeup, paint their nails, coif their hair carefully, and orient to boys. The boys lag behind; although they are also bundles of emerging hormones, they are less interested in girls than girls are in them. However, they begin to construct their gender by playing sports and talking tough, displaying a lunch-table worldliness about cars and sports that signifies their gender (or, more accurately, the gender of their fathers and coaches).

Although memory fades and distorts, I don't remember such elaborate gender rituals in my preteen years. Perhaps I was just out of it! But perhaps the world has gotten faster, as children are more involved than we were in the circuitries of society and sexuality. Their worlds have accelerated because their parents want this for them (or feel helpless to stop it), pushing them out the door to dances and dates, and because kids are inundated by the world, which is at their fingertips after school when they watch television and surf and chat on the Internet. It is nearly impossible not to grow up quickly when exposed to a media culture that displays images of gender, work, class, and race with which to orient young lives. This is a tangled web: Parents acquire gender from the media; they help construct their child's gender, which is redoubled in their peer relations at and after school; and their child's gender is reinforced by the media.

It is no wonder that girls in my daughter's class want to be feminine and fear being labeled lesbian. Indeed, they sanction and punish other girls by calling them lesbians. Boys participate in the same social circuitries, even though they seem "behind" girls in their social self-awareness. Although boys brand as "gay" kids who don't measure up to their relevant gender standard, they are more obtuse about the social significance of gender, perhaps because for men, and by extension boys, their gender is the dominant one; less is at stake for them in the gendered transactions of social power because they already have more power. I think this explains why boys are less involved than girls in a gossip culture, which can be very cruel. This is not because boys are actually "behind" girls in development but because men, who mentor boys to be men, have the upper hand and don't need to define their identities and measure their power with reference to the successful acquisition of gender. Gender just "comes naturally" to boys, or at least appears to do so.

Schoolwork/Adult Work

All parents today know that their kids do more homework than they did. In *The Case against Homework,* Kralovec and Buell (2000) make a reasoned argument against overloading kids with after-school academic work. I agree with much of their argument. It might seem strange that a person with my intellectual orientation would argue against academic pursuits at a moment when our culture is quite anti-intellectual, dominated by a media culture that downgrades intelligence and rewards superficiality. But I am not convinced that piling on homework promotes intellect and enhances an academic culture. Indeed, a faster postmodern capitalism is speeding up childhood to such an extent that we are not only losing the category of the child but also blurring the boundary between children's activities and adult activities: Schoolwork is rapidly becoming like adult work as we expect our kids to, in effect, hold down full-time jobs.

I don't remember homework before junior high. Serious homework didn't commence until high school, if then. My elementary years were largely homework-free. My son started to do homework in first grade. My daughter had at least an hour of homework beginning in the fourth grade. Frequently, in fifth and sixth grade, she had two hours a night. Although her school has a policy of a homework-free weekend, she often does homework on the weekend, especially work on "projects," which abound. I know many other public and private school kids who have the same amounts or more. Parents who care about their kids' school performance are necessarily joined to their kids while they do homework, overseeing and helping where necessary. For my wife and I

96

to check our daughter's seventh-grade prealgebra work, frequently thirty or more problems, takes us an hour, even though we were both quite good in math!

Has homework increased since I was a schoolchild during the late 1950s and 1960s because educational administrators and teachers are concerned about standards and cultural illiteracy? If so, has additional homework made kids better prepared for college? How does student preparation compare to the preparation "we" baby boomers received? I write from the dual perspectives of parent and college professor. Although my kids do more homework than I did growing up in a college town with professorial parents, I don't think their classmates are generally more knowledgeable than we were. Indeed, although they know more facts about Texas history, they arguably know less about the big picture—concepts, cultures, civilizations, and theories. Homework today is coupled with an emphasis on taking tests, especially of the standardized variety, that provide accountability measures in a retrenching public sector. My kids are expected to memorize much more than I did—dates, definitions, species. And they spend less time doing creative writing and other imaginative work, even when they do major science and social studies projects, which are, as much as anything, a test of their parents' social-class background. Affluent parents assist with these projects more than poorer parents, and they provide their kids with intellectual and technological resources with which to complete these projects. It is the parents who are being graded, as all the teachers know.

There is great stress on factual knowledge learned by rote. As a professor, I teach undergraduates who have survived these accelerated K–12 curricula and burdensome homework regimens, and I notice that fact-based elementary school, middle school, and high school curricula have not prepared students well for college, in which speculation, intuition, imagination, and creation are required across the board. Although college students still memorize and do detail work, especially if they enroll in premedical or engineering programs requiring calculus and chemistry classes, their core courses in the liberal arts stress essay writing and term papers, for which my undergraduates are woefully unprepared, having done little real writing in high school and earlier.

My students are fairly good at rote learning but weak at creative thought and writing. Even more telling is that, with only a few exceptions, they aren't intellectually motivated but merely interested in acquiring credentials and earning grades with which to launch their careers and lifestyles. Few students bother to pick up their term papers after I have graded and commented on them. Most students miss a lot of classes unless faculty have stringent attendance policies. This is true even at the graduate level. There is little effort to read beyond the syllabus, even though I tell my classes that I only learned about 10 percent of what I know from actual courses and the written work required in them. Most of my learning was done on my own, in the university library and in my amateur writings, most of which weren't turned in to the professor or eventually published.

Motivation and intellectual curiosity have waned as homework has increased, especially fact-oriented homework. They have been replaced by a *task orientation,* an attention to detail, retention, memorization, timeliness, obedience, and neatness. In their classic jeremiad *Schooling in Capitalist America* (1976), Bowles and Gintis argue that these aspects of a task orientation constitute a "hidden curriculum" preparing students for the adult workplace. I embrace their analysis. However, since the 1970s there has been a speeding up of schooling that doesn't simply prepare students "for" eventual adult work but *becomes* such work as children are viewed and treated, in effect, as adults already. Homework is no longer only preparation but production, a childhood contribution to what Marxists call economic surplus value.

How could this be so? Children don't produce commodities bought and sold in the marketplace. How is their homework productive? It is productive not of commodities but of selves, albeit youthful ones, who eventually play adult roles in work, family, and polity. Marx neglected a social psychology that could explain the connections (he might have called them circuits) among the self, the family, work, and culture that require not only economic objects to be produced but also subjects who conform, consume, and are punctual. This is Bowles and Gintis's argument about the hidden curriculum. But it is not enough to view homework merely as preparation for holding down an office or factory job later in life. Homework should also be seen as immediately productive of selves, K–12 and then college selves, who substitute homework and schoolwork for other activities that could conceivably be threatening to the status quo. Homework is primarily a substitute for *free time,* which a faster capitalism reduces nearly to nothing. Indeed, one could define fast, and then faster, capitalism as an economic and social order in which the scarcest thing of all is time, and hence freedom.

Children are robbed of time, as are adults, so that idle hands don't become the devil's workshop. That is, children and parents with too much time on their hands are distracted, diverted, from the tasks at hand and risk becoming dangerous deviants, even revolutionaries. This is how Marcuse explained that what Freud called "repression" increases as people in post–World War II capitalism taste the prospect of liberation from toil and, thus, from duty. "Surplus" repression prevents people from recognizing that their affluence is an occasion for rethinking capitalism so that not only private life is revalued but also public life, and all the economic and political roles deemed by non-Marxist social theorists to be "necessary" as long as scarcity prevails. The issue for Marcuse was that people with too much time on their hands would opt out of the "performance principle" and give themselves over to the "pleasure principle," which wouldn't be just privatized hedonism but a newfound "rationality of gratification" that overthrows capitalism and positivism.

One historical response to adults having too much time has been to quicken the pace of both public and private life. This was my argument fifteen years ago. But this now extends into childhood, which a post-Fordist postmodern capitalism is on the verge of undoing. Children are denied time previously off limits to social engineering so that when they become adults, or even college students, they have abandoned the pleasure principle and, with it, utopia. As I have remarked, my daughter's classmates are already formulating college, career, and lifetime plans. They think they know where they will go to college, which in Texas, for middle-class kids, is reduced to a short list of in-state schools. They think they know what kind of car they will drive, where they will live, what they will do, how many children and pets they will have. Although some or all of these things may change, as they always do, it is notable that kids are planning their lives, and their careers, in adultlike ways, the pleasure principle having been drummed out of them by the time they reach middle school let alone their first real job.

This is certainly an aspect of Bowles and Gintis's hidden curriculum in that massive amounts of homework designed to suck up kids' time is preparation for an adulthood of too much to do and too little time to do it. But this goes beyond preparation for vocation. In a faster capitalism, time is robbed from children in order to extinguish hope and yearning, the utopian impulse. Kids, in their nature, exist in an idealized (if not always ideal) world of freedom from constraint, which is expressed in their play. The play impulse is a crucial component of the pleasure principle, expressing an instinct for loosely structured but aimless fun, including but not limited to competition. Although it could be argued that becoming an adult involves learning limits and how to delay gratification, childhood is developmentally distinct from adulthood precisely in that kids dream and play without much limit.

Childhood is so important because children understand how to play and how to achieve pleasure. They inhabit a kind of utopia, even though it is not politically institutionalized or even known to adults. Childhood can be cruel, too, especially during adolescence, as cliques form and bullying takes place. But I would argue that kids learn from their parents and from the culture how to exclude and include and how to bully and browbeat. These are not inherent in our natures but residues of a history that bears witness to recurring hierarchy, which is internalized through the social psychology and stratification systems of children's and teenagers' informal hierarchies. Kids in their nature are egalitarian, auguring a utopia without distinctions. They learn how to distinguish, to sort, to exclude, to label because they watch their parents and their cultural heroes do that.

The speedup of childhood and adolescence is inseparable from overall acceleration, for adults as well as their kids. Time compresses under sway of administration because capitalism needs people to forget how to play, dream, and enjoy idle time. Sebastian DeGrazia understood this well in his *Of Time, Work and Leisure* (1962). What happens to children, and their parents, is twofold: People have "less" time because too many activities fill their waking hours and reduce their sleep. And these waking hours are scheduled with the help of planners, Palm Pilots, and calendars (both pulp and electronic). Time has undergone further *periodization* since Frederick Taylor first understood the conversion of time and motion into capital. Taylor and Henry Ford authored the scientific management of work and, thus, of time. But when they wrote and worked, during the early twentieth century, the hours susceptible to periodization and administration were far fewer than they are today. Taylor regimented the working day for adults, not their leisure time and not the time use of children.

Taylor and Ford felt that it was important for capitalism to regulate time, at least work time, so that workers would be productive. The regulation of work time began during the early Industrial Revolution. Workers did not have watches or clocks, and their employers rang bells to indicate starting and stopping time. Workers had to trust them to tell the time correctly. Personal time was not kept, as most people continued to regulate their nonwork activities with respect to the seasons and to sunrise and sunset, the typical pattern of timekeeping from antiquity through the Middle Ages. Taylor and Ford took timekeeping to another level because they were convinced that labor could become even more productive if workers' every move was calculated, measured, analyzed.

Today, the office and plant have been rationalized far beyond Taylor and Ford's wildest imaginings. Every action is subject to the rule of calculation, supervision, surveillance, and prediction. This is what Weber both praised and disparaged as the "rationalization" of the world (Weber 1978). He felt it was inescapable, if somewhat lamentable, given the toll in human meanings, values, and creativity. Marx and later the Frankfurt School linked rationalization and capitalism, noticing that work came under the rule and regime of calculation and time management precisely to benefit capital and not humanity. I have argued, and am arguing even more emphatically here, that capitalism has intensified the management of time and motion, extending far beyond the workplace to include leisure and even dreaming. Employers can even track their employees' Internet use.

Examples abound in the worlds of both adults and children. Our lives seem so "busy" because we cram too many activities into daytime and nighttime affairs. A primary activity, chewing up time and motion in itself, is the balancing of work and family, which is primarily a woman's activity. The majority of American women now work, but they are still responsible for the management of the household and especially of children. I recently asked my wife why there weren't more dads at our kids' elementary school carnival, which was held at the end of the day. She replied, "Because women 'do' kids." Going to the carnival, for many of these moms, involved a lot of work and planning—time. Perhaps they worked one of the carnival booths, for which they needed preparation and possibly a committee meeting or two. Perhaps they have an older child, at a different school, whose after-school care would need to be addressed by someone else. And who was going to prepare dinner after a hot and tiring afternoon?

Just as moms' lives are periodized and administered, so are their children's lives. The kids get picked up from school, confronting an hour or more of homework. They have after-school music lessons and sports practices. Their weekends are crowded with more homework, games, recitals, and birthday parties. They stay up later than I remember staying up as a kid. For kids entering adolescence, sleep deprivation is a real problem, as it is for many adults, who regularly stay up too late and awaken too early, and may have troubled sleep in between. Kids are taught to accelerate: At my daughter's junior high, students are allowed a meager five minutes between classes, during which they must move from class to class and use the bathroom. If they are late to class, they are "locked out" of the classroom and they must attend Saturday school as punishment. In protest to the vice principal I characterized this approach to young bodies in motion as like a "penal colony." Kids increasingly live like adults: They get as little sleep, and they face crammed schedules and adultlike expectations of performance, performativity (attention to task), and acceleration.

We are in effect eliminating childhood, or at least abbreviating it, as we turn children's activities into work and performance and subject them to regulation, periodization, and administration. The developmental segue from childhood to adulthood is being blurred not to make adult life more playful and carefree but to rob youth of its purposive purposelessness, its joie de vivre, its frivolity. We are doing this, as I said, not simply to *prepare* children for adulthood but to *substitute* adulthood for childhood. We are doing this because there is concern that children are "too" free and might never learn discipline and domination. And children's utopian imagination of a perfect classless, raceless, borderless world is threatening to the adults surrounding them, who have long since given up playfulness and praxis in order to "function" in a world of rules and hierarchy. The presence of children reminds their parents and teachers how unfree they are, and they resent it.

Resentment and jealousy are hallmarks of authoritarianism, as the Frankfurt School showed. We have accelerated childhood, in effect attenuating it, because adults have had their own lives accelerated and administered and they resent children for having it too easy. Adorno and his coworkers in the *Authoritarian Personality* project (Adorno et al. 1950) argued that catastrophes such as the Holocaust happened because people followed tyrants in order to fulfill their own needs for identification with a powerful father figure. Authoritarianism thus involves the exercise of both top-down authority and bottom-up subordination. The authoritarian leader mobilizes people's feelings of inadequacy and alienation and directs them toward resented and feared Others, such as Jews or homosexuals, thus deflecting attention from himself. The Frankfurt School viewed fascism as "total administration," the subjection of all public and personal life to manipulation and management. Although it is risky to characterize too much homework and too little time to play as fascist, politicians, parents, and teachers who would attenuate childhood do so out of needs such as low self-esteem and alienation similar to the needs motivating people throughout history to join in the persecution of even weaker Others. Children are the new Others, the new Jews and homosexuals, in a faster capitalism.

VIRTUAL SELVES

One of the crucial insights of the Frankfurt School is that the family in capitalism has lost many of its functions as a civilizing, socializing, and sheltering institution. Many feminists would respond that the patriarchal, male-run family never performed these roles and thus cannot accurately be characterized as a haven. The family was always a little workshop in which women "produce" children, affection, meals, and sex, albeit outside of the wage relationship. I view both of these perspectives, however contradictory, as correct: The family, like childhood, has been dangerously abbreviated, and the male-run family should not be idealized as a benchmark against which social progress can be measured.

French postmodern theory, especially the work of Foucault, helps integrate these theoretical perspectives on family. Foucault, although sympathetic to Marxism, is not a Marxist because he rejects economic determinism. Foucault addresses power and domination as they reside in small gestures and daily discourses, even in the learning of penmanship (1977). He realizes, as do critical theorists, that social control has invaded people's psyches and bodies, that it is not something simply imposed on them from the outside. It is both imposed and self-imposed, involving the person in his or her own domination.

This helps postmodern theorists, especially feminist ones like Foucault, address the family both as a site of oppression and as a sheltered harbor. Foucault helps us see that the family (nor patriarchy, nor the acceleration of life) is not simply imposed on us but is partly a choice and partly a discursive positioning, which is a technical way of saying that we are born into a world in which people "do" family in certain ways because the frameworks with which we are brought up limit our choices and narrow our horizons. Postmodernism, existentialism, and phenomenology all help us understand social structure's impact on selves and selves' impact on social structure, which is much the same point made by Marx when he said that people are both products and authors of their history.

The family, therefore, is a dialectical phenomenon, sometimes entrapping people and sometimes sheltering and humanizing them (see Zaretsky 1976). Indeed, there is no single "family" but numerous different versions, as many types of family, it seems, as there are families. When I talk of the virtual family I am pointing to the ways in which the thin boundaries between private and public life are becoming even more permeable by information technologies, sexual politics, and the transformation and truncation of childhood. This is "virtual" because it is largely through television, telephones, and the Internet that we are losing the ability to shut out the world, which bears down heavily on us and robs us of space and time to recover let alone think imaginatively about alternative social arrangements. Postmodern theory helps us understand the blurring of boundaries between and among social institutions, such as work and family and family and education—and of course media—thus requiring us to theorize selves and everyday life, especially childhood, in ways typically ignored by mainstream male social theory and social science.

Feminists have always understood that the personal is political. And they paid attention to children as actors not yet fully able to make life-defining choices, except bad ones, as they behave like adults before they can handle the consequences. One of my daughter's classmates, a bright girl from a well-educated family, recently told the class that she "wants to get laid," occasioning numerous rumors and eventually getting back to her mother, who promptly "grounded" her. *Grounding* is a way of closing off the world, functioning both physically and metaphorically to slow down childhood. It is not always understood as such by parents who don't understand their children's shortcomings and transgressions theoretically but who instead merely want to see them punished so that, in biblical terms, they are morally rectified.

Critical theory's ambivalence about the family is instructive. On the one hand, I agree with Habermas and many feminists that social forces located in the public sphere invade the family and even the self. These social forces need to be blunted so that private autonomy can be restored or gained and so that the family can be a nurturing counterweight to

106

public domination. But on the other hand, critical theory, beginning with Marx, regrets what some theorists call "privatization," the demise of the public sphere and an ensuing shallow individualism of shopping and entertainment. Here, Marxist-inspired theorists, and many left-wing feminists as well, are noticing a fundamental tension between democracy (of the New England town meeting and Paris Commune) and capitalism. Capitalism thwarts democracy where it denies people opportunities to enter from private life into a public sphere in which they can regulate their own affairs, all the way from politics and economics to culture and education.

As the New Left emphasized, democracy requires both healthy social institutions and selves capable of participating in public life. The boundaried family is the social institution positioned to nurture democratic selves who become social and political activists. It is also supposed to nurture people who tire of public life, especially of work, and need to be restored. Today, as feminists and critical theorists note, the family has become merely a factory in which diligent children and needy adult materialists are produced. It is neither a haven nor a platform for democratic projects. Feminist historians maintain that the patriarchal family has never been a safe harbor for women and children, and thus they refrain from glorifying the mythical nuclear family of lore. But things have gotten worse for women and children, and even for men, as we have entered the era of post-Fordist virtuality in which families are swamped by an Internet and media culture, by homework, and by the variety of children's organized activities.

Families, even imperfect patriarchal or single-parent ones, have become virtual, held together by cell phones, the Internet, fast food, television, rented movies, and videos. Face-to-face families, however inadequate from a feminist and Frankfurt School perspective, provided people sustenance, meaning, mentorship, and direction. People before the 1990s spent more time together and thus helped build decent social relationships and selves; they were less privatized. Today, families "chat" over the Internet instead of with each other, just as they eat separately. This has the advantage of keeping people in contact, both talking and writing (via e-mail). This has the disadvantage of privatizing them in their cubicles, offices, and bedrooms as they stare at computer screens and try to remember what the human voice and touch felt like.

This is especially troubling for children, who grow up too fast, inundated by the world that electronically encroaches on their busy days, and on their psyches, too. Virtual children risk not being children at all, as they possess a worldliness not matched by an adequate repertoire of social skills and intellectual development. Almost by definition, virtual selves and their virtual children are not selves at all but pastiches, assemblages, of electronic stimuli that fill our airwaves and coaxial cables with discourse and images encouraging us to configure our identities in system-serving ways, as shoppers, citizens, parents, and workers. The world is too much with us, especially with our children, in an era of virtuality that, as I am arguing here, is not disconnected from capitalism but instead is its postmodern, post-Fordist, post-twentieth-century extension.

Where the family is concerned, and the family's children, we can use the Internet to make the work/family connection seamless, to lighten the homework burden, to encourage skeptical inquiry as opposed to blind faith. There is nothing wrong with technology, including information and entertainment technologies, if we understand that technology is not a deus ex machina, possessing an inherent goodness or evil, but a literary project, an authorial outcome, that can be laid bare for its hidden assumptions and political implications. Parents who worry about their selves, and particularly their children's selves, need to understand the erosion of the public/private boundary and its impact on children and childhood in theoretical terms, helping them make good decisions about whether to allow their kids to enter chat rooms, to watch evening television, to play video games, to download popular music. These parents—we—need to understand what is at stake in a virtual capitalism, a faster capitalism than the one I addressed before the Internet: What is at stake is the self, and our kids' selves, the public sphere and private life. Virtuality is neither to be celebrated nor condemned without thinking theoretically, dialectically, about the interaction between the pace and space of social life, on the one hand, and our technologies, on the other. The fact that I am composing this book on our home computer while listening to a music CD is not lost on me: I am participating in, as well as analyzing, an unprecedented stage of world history in which familiar institutional distinctions among work, office, home, leisure, adulthood, and childhood have been turned on their head as we have anytime/anywhere access to information technologies.

5

Fast Food, Fasting Bodies

The term "fast" is used as an adjective to connote quickened time and as a noun to indicate a period without eating. In this chapter, I examine how our fast lives are sustained by fast food, causing us to fast and exercise. This is a genuinely dialectical phenomenon, containing contradiction and possible synthesis, which is, according to Hegel and Marx, the moving force of history. I explore the disciplining implications of diet and exercise as well as their gendered characteristics. I also turn the tables by suggesting ways in which the body is a contested terrain, not only a site of "fast" domination but also a battleground on which selves resist their disciplining and create a new, "slower" order of things, what I call slow-modernity in my concluding chapter. This is a particularly feminist agenda, demonstrating vividly that the personal—body, diet, exercise, fashion, makeup—is political, even though it doesn't exhaust politics (see Agger 1993).

Fast Food, Feasting Bodies

In a faster capitalism people are preoccupied with work and rush around to insert their fragile family lives into a 24/7 workday, joined to the workplaces by instantaneizing information technologies. Indeed, I am writing these words early on a Saturday evening (6:41 p.m., to be exact), while my son plays games on his PlayStation 2 with a friend upstairs and my wife and daughter attend a birthday party at an electronic arcade. As I noted earlier, I am not the ordinary wage slave under the thumb of a boss. I am sandwiching a few moments writing in between my kids' softball and baseball games, my own tennis matches, catching a bass in the backyard creek, making dinner, and preparing to watch game seven of the Dallas Mavericks playoff series against Sacramento with my son and his friend later in the evening.

I'm not above eating out, indeed I love to go to a funky Mexican restaurant in a converted garage. But my work's inherent flexibility and lack of accountability allow me time and energy to cook and exercise. I need to watch my consumption of fat and to keep my "good" cholesterol high by working out. I've always fashioned myself an athlete, having nearly broken three hours in the marathon. And I play tennis every day, at least when I'm not injured from playing too much! I have time during the day to play tennis and lift weights. And I can spend time planning my family's diet and preparing food for all of us. My wife, one of the nation's experts in the sociology of housework, will attest that I do less than my share of "domestic labor," for which I am eternally guilty, but at least I am working on such issues! I have ample *time* on my hands, which I can spend on self-care, staying in shape, eating well, and hanging out with my kids and wife (who is a frequent tennis and lunch partner).

By comparison to most other wage slaves in America, I lead a slow life. Although my family has a home computer and some CDs, we don't have a fancy plasma or big-screen TV. Until quite recently, we had only one television. Our kids have PlayStation2 but few other technological paraphernalia. And they don't "chat" with friends on the Internet. My wife and I can afford to be healthy, and keep our family healthy, because we have flexible jobs and—again!—time. We can slow things down and keep the world at bay because we don't work forty hours a week in a cubicle or factory. Our kids don't need after-school care. We experience little stress, and we both have low blood pressure.

This demonstrates, again, that we can't either demonize or lionize technologies such as the Internet and computers, which make my occupational flexibility and productivity possible. It all depends on how they are used. This is true of all "convenience" technologies, which are a topic of this chapter. I am particularly interested in *technologies of the body,* involving food, eating, dieting, and exercising (see Foucault 1977; O'Neill 1985). For the most part, these are "fast" technologies, and they are getting faster. "Fast" foods, "fast" food restaurants, "fast" diets, and "fast" exercise programs and equipment all promise acceleration of bodies—bodies in motion. There is nothing inherently evil about fast food if that food is healthy, eaten convivially, and inexpensive, and does not contribute to suburban sprawl. But I have not just described McDonald's or Wendy's, as Eric Schlosser makes clear in his *Fast Food Nation* (2001), an indictment of fast food and of the slaughterhouses that supply hamburger chains.

Why "fast" food? From the establishment of the McDonald's chain, which began as a single restaurant in the San Bernardino Valley during the late 1940s and early 1950s, there was an inextricable link between fast food and fast cars. There was also a link between working and eating. Henry Ford made affordable automobiles available to Americans, and President Dwight Eisenhower oversaw the development of an interstate highway system. Although an obvious utility for travel to and from work, driving, as Kay (1997) indicates, was also about freedom on the open road, culminating in the mythology of Route 66. In particular, cars could take people away from the uninviting asphalt jungle of the busy Fordist city, which was as yet ungentrified. By the late 1940s, Americans had begun to use cars to fill leisure time, as well as for commuting. Drive-in restaurants were made to order for an emerging asphalt nation. The McDonald brothers got the bright idea that drive-ins could serve inexpensive food in a traditional restaurant setting, promising, above all, cheap cost and timely service. It took Ray Kroc, who bought this "idea" from the McDonalds, to franchise these cheap roadside hamburger restaurants, following in the footsteps of his World War I buddy Walt Disney, who understood that Americans wanted to enjoy their leisure in the simulation of small-town America called Disneyland. Eventually, McDonald's gained a monopoly in Disney's original amusement park, wedding themed food and themed amusement.

By *theming* I am referring to a total experience of escape promised by an amusement park, a shopping mall, a restaurant organized around a unifying idea (see Gottdiener 1997). There was always a certain utopian intention in the brainchildren of Kroc and Disney, who recognized that people were alienated in their day jobs and in stultifying cities and suburbs and that they yearned to escape. Disney promised time travel back to the bucolic small town with manageable dimensions and no cars. Kroc promised the family experience of dining while on the road, minimizing the expenditure of both time and money. Both "themes" were standardized, suggesting a fungibility of experience. You can patronize Disney's utopia on both coasts and eat at the thousands of McDonald's franchises in between with the expectation that a themed, branded experience is fundamentally similar everywhere. Although by the twenty-first century savvy fast-food franchisers recognize that people like local flavor, especially as these franchises sprout outside the United States, Kroc and Disney understood that people want the safety and the security of look-alike franchises.

Fast food appeals not only to people on the run, and on route, but also to people who seek standardization, captured in theming, in a world that is jumbled and chaotic. Baudrillard's (1983) perspectives on "simulation" help us understand this better, especially where we consider the role of advertising in the fast-food experience. Food franchisers advertise their products relentlessly, as anyone who watches television knows. There are two levels of simulation going on: First, the advertising presents real people (although we know they are actors, a third level of simulation) eating at McDonald's. They are happy and carefree, and they love the food, which looks appetizing. Thus, patronage is simulated by the advertising campaign. Also simulated is the sense of escape and release, of utopia, occasioned by eating out. One goes to McDonald's and other fast-food chains not only for food and toys for the kids but for a total experience of family, friendship, and neighborhood that is increasingly absent from people's lives.

The simulation of family and community is especially important as people's lives have gotten busier, or accelerated, as I prefer to term it. Eating out at "fast" restaurants contradictorily promises efficiency and alacrity, on the one hand, and a rupture in the continuum of domination, on the other. Brisk Taylorized food production is curiously mixed with Disney-like yearning for yesteryear and for family. It is not enough to notice that people began to eat a lot of fast food when they began driving and their work lives got busier. Fast-food patronage also involves cathexis and catharsis, a break from the everyday even as the everyday is standardized and simulated.

The McDonald brothers, Kroc, and Disney began their pioneering work of standardizing food production and entertainment and then franchising and theming them over half a century ago. By now, the Golden Arches and Disney logos are part of the quotidian environment, taken for granted by everyone who drives, travels, shops for children's toys, and watches television. Fast food and fast entertainment have become routine, "routinized" to use Weber's term. (For a discussion of "McDonaldization" from Weber's perspective, see Ritzer 1993.) Two things have happened in the meantime: People experience a widening gap between the advertising simulation of the idyllic franchised experience and the actual product, and people have become habituated to eating and living like this, especially inasmuch as advertising, for more than a generation, has been pitched to children and adolescents. It is taken for granted that lunch or dinner means a hamburger, not one cooked on the backyard grill but a paper-wrapped or Styrofoam-encased version covered with brands.

Now that fast food and even Disney parks have become routine, their utopianizing function is less easily achieved. Visit a fast-food chain restaurant, whether McDonald's, Burger King, or Wendy's, and you are likely to find a less-than-immaculate restaurant staffed by somewhat sullen and not very competent suburban or inner-city kids. The food is likely to be lackluster, having reposed in warming bins. The servers may have gotten your order wrong, even after you have waited in line (or in your car) for longer than the word "fast" suggests. The children's play area, crucial for the utopian image of a playful wonderland somehow separate from every-day life, is likely to be dirty and have broken play equipment.

A certain degradation has accompanied the routinization of the fast-food experience. The first McDonald's that opened in my hometown of Eugene, Oregon, back in the late 1960s was a thrilling departure from our parents' boring restaurants. A high school friend who had a car would give us a ride to the Golden Arches. The fries were delicious, and we were amazed at the low cost of the hamburgers—just 19 cents! Big Macs were a tasty novelty, and our veins weren't yet clogged with cholesterol. The local McDonald's franchise in Eugene wasn't yet themed to signify family, community, utopia. It wasn't a simulation produced by advertising, whereby the consump-tion of its logos substituted for the consumption of dubiously edible burgers. Instead, the Eugene McDonald's was a gather-ing point for teenagers who experienced real sociality, real society, in its parking lots and in its booths. In this sense, the 1969 McDonald's of my youth was like the 1950s diners of *American Graffiti* lore and not the drab franchises of the early twenty-first century, where the food is bad, the servers sullen, and Ronald McDonald a big stuffed dummy.

Why, then, does patronage of fast-food restaurants persist? Official restaurant ideology suggests that people like the food, find it appropriately economical, and want to save time when on the road and on the run. But, in fact, patronage at American fast-food restaurants has declined over the past decade; what industry growth there is occurs in an international market in which such franchises signify modernity in nations "behind" the United States in modernization, such as Russia and China. American patronage has declined for several reasons. There are other affordable casual-dining options, such as Denny's and Luby's. People are turned off by bad food and alienated, low-wage servers. The restaurants don't deliver the promised utopia of family and community. Finally, people are concerned about the health implications of high-fat, high-salt diets. McDonald's and its competitors have tried to forestall this by advertising "healthy" culinary options such as salads and chicken sandwiches. But again there are higher-quality options, such as Subway, which is the fastest growing casual-eating chain in the United States. Subway has seized the day by positioning itself as the brand for dieters, running advertisements showing huge weight loss for patrons who subsisted on a steady diet of low-fat Subway sandwiches. At Subway, unlike most of the hamburger chains, the sandwiches are made to order in full view of the customer, giving the impression of a higher-quality dining experience.

EXORCISING/EXERCISING THE FAST BODY

Fast food makes you fat because it is laden with fat. And obesity in America is rampant and rapidly spreading. Fast food is addictive, as are many fatty and salty foods. Also addictive is the ease with which fast food can be consumed, without having to cook the food and wash the dishes. Eating fast food and other heavily refined prepared foods dulls the taste buds and makes fresh, home-cooked food taste weird. And, at the end of the day, a steady diet of fast foods and refined foods requires one to exercise, fast! There is a dialectic, which is telling, of fast food and fasting, positioning what I am calling the fast body as a political site of contradiction, conflict, and consciousness.

The fast/feasting/fasting body needs to diet and exercise in order to exorcise the effects of an unhealthy diet and lifestyle, including the lack of exercise. All of these things are interconnected; they form what Hegel called a totality. We rush around, spending little time together cooking and eating. We grab fast food, on the run and on the road, and then become habituated to eating it. No kid wants pinto beans with rice and fresh broccoli when she has grown up eating chicken nuggets and french fries. This can lead to obesity, even in children, especially if we relax during our precious down time by lying on the couch watching TV or sitting while playing video games and surfing the Web. By some estimates, a third of American kids are obese or on their way to being so. And fewer than a quarter of adults get enough exercise for their well-being.

What happens to the fast body that eats poorly, doesn't exercise, gets insufficient sleep, and perhaps drinks too much? All told, longevity, or life expectancy, is diminished by these various risk factors. And these lifestyle choices lead to a greater risk of serious illness, such as high blood pressure, stroke, and heart attack. As capitalism accelerates, the fast body also accelerates, buffeted by the ill winds of industry and the culture industry, doing things to itself that aren't healthy in service of profit and as an effect of time compression.

False needs and inadequate self-care are both imposed on people and self-imposed, under sway of advertising and culture. No one holds a gun to our heads, or our kids', when we bundle into the car in search of a double cheeseburger and greasy fries, washed down by a Coke, a meal that is high in calories, fat, and caffeine and very low in nutritional value. Capitalists respond to manipulated taste by providing more of the same: Morality lies in giving people what they want, even if those wants are bad for them and expensive for society as a whole because health-care costs rapidly escalate. Capitalists do their share in manipulating people's tastes, which are internalized as free choices by people who appear to have many options—where and what to eat, what to do in leisure time, how much or how little to exercise, how many alcoholic beverages to drink. Kids ape parents, who ape the culture as a whole, and especially their media culture heroes. And unless we are self-sufficient or live in towns and cities with organic-food stores, we seem trapped by what's available at the local Safeway or Albertsons, which, as every student of marketing will attest, simply reflects what people purchased last quarter and the quarter before that.

The fast body not only eats the wrong foods and disdains aerobic exercise for at least thirty minutes two or three times a week; she also exposes herself to too much stress, which is a silent killer of both women and men. Students of life expectancy such as actuaries and demographers well understand that stress weakens people's immune systems and assaults their hearts. And stress relief too often takes the form of overeating, eating junk food, drinking, drugs, both licit (tobacco) and illicit (marijuana and cocaine), and sedentary television viewing. Exercise is a healthier way to relax, and it reduces "bad" cholesterol and increases "good" cholesterol.

By the time people, especially men, begin to realize what is happening to their bodies, it can be too late. Years of overeating, too much cholesterol, lack of exercise, drinking, and possibly smoking have laid waste to the prime of their lives. At that point—and of course this applies to women, too—they try to reverse the downward spiral: They, in effect, fast, or rather they embark on fast fixes, such as weight loss programs and crash diets. As anyone knows who has wandered around a Barnes & Noble or GNC store lately, the diet industry is vast and growing, judging by the books, tapes, and chemical elixirs available. The Atkins diet prescribes lots of protein and almost no carbohydrates, whereas Jenny Craig relies on counseling and its own prepared foods. The few good diets available, such as Pritikin (1979), recommend life-long healthy eating, such as a reduction in saturated fat and trans fats and an increase in complex carbohydrates mixed with strenuous aerobic exercise.

People resolve to shed weight and get more exercise, especially after the holidays. They begin diets and join gyms or purchase exercise equipment. For some, these additions (or are they deletions?) actually work, triggering long-term lifestyle changes. For most, they merely increase credit card debt and erode self-esteem. After decades of indolence and indulgence, it is difficult to change not only one's habits but also one's identity. It is virtually impossible to engage in hard-core daily exercise, whether or not this leads to competition, without eating well. If you don't view yourself as an athlete, you cannot become one. Walking a few times around the block and then going home to refined, prepared foods (or out to a mainstream restaurant) is a waste of time, especially for people in their forties and beyond who have clogged their arteries with cholesterol and larded their bodies with fat. Although it is never too late for anyone to reverse these trends, fast dieting and exercising are futile and, indeed, they are components of an accelerated life lived thoughtlessly and without plan.

Fast food produces fasting as people attempt to exorcise bad habits and heal damaged bodies. It isn't fasting exactly but crash dieting, abetted by costly guides, prepared foods, and sometimes drugs. We have established two industries that seem contradictory but, under faster capitalism, have become complementary: the fat-laden fast-food and prepared foods industries, on the one hand, and the diet and exercise indus-tries, on the other. We eat too much and we eat the wrong things, and then we crash diet and embark on ill-conceived short-term exercise and weight-loss routines. Either way, we are the poorer for it.

Am I Thin Enough Yet? Fasting Feminine Bodies

As Hesse-Biber (1996) has shown in her study of college-age American women, you can't be thin enough. Male college students in her study were for the most part happy with the way they look in the mirror. This is about gender, the ways in which men and women develop their identities, bodies, and behavior as either "masculine" or "feminine." Body politics, involving what I call the fast body, torments women much more than men, as Hesse-Biber and numerous feminist scholars have shown. Fat is a feminist issue because women have been trained, from earliest childhood, to define themselves in terms of their attractiveness to men, which, in our Victorian culture, involves an impossibly slender female form coupled with protuberant breasts.

Thinness is culturally attractive in our male-run culture because thin women are childlike and thus seem less powerful and threatening to men. I recently watched a "reality television" show in which twenty or so women competed for the hand of a male, who then proposed marriage. Most of the contestants were in their twenties and thus missed the feminist revolution of the 1960s and 1970s. On the episode that I sampled, a woman, who was conventionally attractive and in no way overweight, anticipated that she couldn't compete successfully against the other women because they were "so small." She elaborated that they had "great bodies," implying that she was big and unattractive. She was saying, in effect, that their bodies looked like the bodies of young girls. I had to look closely to appreciate the distinction between "small" and "big" and it was hard to see what she was talking about. They all looked pretty much the same—conventionally attractive, not overweight, carefully coiffed, with lots of makeup. And they all talked in the Generation-X patois of Drew Barrymore and Reese Witherspoon, which feigns stupidity and emphasizes childishness. Big, small, in between, these women were basically airheads whose major challenge in life was getting their hair and makeup just right. And the man for whom they were competing was equally doltish.

Watching this episode make me feel old, a relic from the 1960s, when women didn't shave their legs and called themselves women, not girls or chicks, as women often do today. One of the slogans of the postfeminist generation is "chicks rock," unwittingly applying a sexist term for women to themselves. Feminism, which I am increasingly convinced was restricted to the generation of young women who came of age during the 1960s, has given way to femininity, which reaches back to Victorianism for images of slender, prettified women adorning and sculpting themselves to be attractive to heterosexual men. Why would women want to be attractive to men? Today, my preteen daughter's friends and my college students, only a decade older, would respond that it should be obvious: women want to "get" a man, to whom they will be wed. The distinction, which is really a dichotomy, between masculine and feminine is grounded in the Victorian, male-ruled family in which a sharp differentiation between the sexes conceals sharp inequalities of wealth, power, and citizenship. In other words, the Victorians removed women from factory work so they could tend the household, children, and even the husband, creating different roles for them than for their husbands, who were breadwinners. To accomplish this, they needed to persuade women and men to view themselves differently, to develop different *gender identities,* that is, how they see themselves as sexual beings.

Women were supposed to be sensitive, caring, empathetic, and nurturing, whereas men were supposed to be calculating, instrumental, strategic, and brave. Women were supposed to be moms, and men dads, soldiers, workers, athletes. The feminist movement begun by Simone de Beauvoir and Betty Friedan argued that women and men aren't biologically, naturally suited to different roles than women but, rather, these role differences and differences in sensibility are historical, products of certain political, social, and sexual arrangements

121

that can be changed. Both authors, and others like Germaine Greer and Gloria Steinem, believe that it is permissible, indeed valuable, for women to get college degrees and work outside the home. As I noted earlier, later scholars such as Nancy Chodorow (1978) argued that it is unhealthy for little boys and girls to be raised by a mom who stays home while the dad, out working, is absent. This leads boys, who need to extricate themselves from the mom's apron strings, to shun intimacy, and it leads girls to reproduce their mother's subordination in the household, economy, and polity. Feminists who focus on family relationships and roles urge shared parenting and a more equal household division of labor.

What has happened to feminism in the meantime? A faster capitalism has caused women born after 1970 to forget the struggles and gains of their mothers and older sisters; they experience amnesia, forgetting of the past, as they live in the moment, self-absorbed and self-regarding (see Baumgardner and Richards 2000). Generation X and Y women (and, of course, men who never supported feminism) reach back to earlier conceptions of femininity, gender identity, the household, parenting, and the body that deviate little from the Victorians' image of the powerless, corseted, mothering woman. These generations are sometimes labeled postfeminist, although that mistakenly implies that they have learned from feminism and no longer need its strident sexual politics. Chicks rock, and girls rule.

One major difference between the Victorians and postfeminists is that it is now perfectly acceptable for young women to attend college and then embark on careers. Indeed, a species of feminist theory and politics called liberal feminism suggests that women will make gains by finding jobs, changing laws governing women's reproductive rights, and bargaining rationally with their husbands and bosses for a fair deal (see Jaggar 1983). Although more radical feminists don't object to this agenda as such, they go further, often much further, to question not only women staying home but the very concept of gender inasmuch as it underpins women's inequality by marking out separate sensibilities, and thus behaviors, for women and men. These more radical feminists argue that gender is a prison because it tells women and men how to act out their sexuality in differing, and even opposing, ways, with men "strong" and women "weak" and needy.

A central issue in this debate between liberal and radical feminists is the politics of the body and of sexuality. For the most part, liberal feminists and postfeminists argue that women are destined to be with men, to have sex with them, to bear their children, to differentiate their sensibilities from men's. In this light, it is okay for them to make themselves attractive to men, which is culturally defined in terms of past precedent and perhaps even biology. That is, certain physical characteristics are judged to be more attractive to the opposite sex than other characteristics, and thus women and even men position themselves and their bodies in the dating and mating marketplace accordingly. Much of this derived from Victorianism, which set a standard of femininity that still endures: small waists, prominent breasts, makeup, managed hair, perfume, dresses, stockings, and so on. In other words, liberal feminists think it is all right for women to adorn themselves and shape their bodies for men, whether they believe that heterosexual attractiveness stems from nature (our hormones and the way they inform our vision) or nurture (cultural standards of beauty).

Radical feminists oppose sharply differentiated categories of femininity and masculinity and the standards of beauty and body positionings that derive from them. They argue for greater "androgyny," which means a less-sharp differentiation, and perhaps even the elimination of all differentiation, between the sexes. By this standard, women can be "masculine," wear pants, do "male" jobs, play sports, shed makeup and perfume. And men can be empathetic, do housework, raise kids, and wear shorts and ankle socks. (A female, a liberal-feminist colleague, once told me that my sports anklets were "fruity." A neighbor, probably not a feminist at all, said that on their first date her prospective husband made the fashion mistake of wearing a pink shirt, which she read as "faggy.")

Radical feminists not only don't endorse Victorian standards of feminine beauty and body positioning but also view corseting and thinness as male-inspired power plays that devalue women by infantilizing them—making women look like girls. Feminist cultural studies notices that the very appellation "girl" when applied to adult women is a power play that, like the word "chick," devalues and diminishes women. It is apparent that 1960s feminism has given way to a Generation X and Y postfeminism, replacing the slogans "the personal is political" and "our bodies, ourselves" with "girl power."

Radical/cultural feminist critique pays special attention to the pathologies of excessive thinness that leads to, and reflects, eating disorders such as bulimia and anorexia nervosa that are themselves power plays imposed and self-imposed on women unhappy with their bodies. "Am I thin enough yet?" "Will guys want to date and marry me?" "Do I look feminine or like a dyke?" "Are my ankles too fat?" "Is my butt too big?" "Will botox remove my wrinkles?" "Is that dress flattering?" This is the discourse of postfeminist women such as those interviewed by Hesse-Biber (1996) in her study of college women struggling with the politics of the body and food. These women tell poignant narratives of their mothers' influence on them, their own low self-esteem, their coping strategies such as binge eating followed by starvation diets and perhaps even purging, their calculus of dating and mating. Hesse-Biber argues that self-hatred is involved in this body positioning that stresses thinness above all else. She reads this as a male power play in the sense that men secretly want women to dislike themselves so that they will be more pliant in their relations with men, more likely to have sex with men and to bear their children and do the dishes. The problem is that many women and men don't recognize the politics of bodies for what it is but thoughtlessly enact gender dramas scripted for them by parents, peers, and our media culture.

My daughter's friends don't know any better. Most of them have moms who aren't feminists, even if many of them work. They dutifully took the husband's last name when they married. They teach their daughters to want marriage, to snag a man. Their moms beautify them, teaching them the arts of makeup, dressing, shopping, eating, and dieting. My daughter's friends talk about "dieting" and "working out"; some even go to the gym to firm their abs. The majority wear makeup and shave their legs. Their homeroom voted a particular girl, who is preternaturally mature, "prettiest" and "best dressed" (this latter even though all kids at her school wear school uniforms).

In the 1960s feminists identified fat as a feminist issue, recognizing that Victorian standards of beauty and thinness were imposed on women by men who wanted to control them—even to starve them (see Bordo 1993). Today the body has been removed from politics, from the body politic, by postfeminists who value femininity as well as certain feminist goals such as equal pay for equal work. These women, especially those born after the 1960s, such as our daughters and students, objectify themselves as well as embrace their male objectification. They stare at themselves in the mirror, giving in to self-absorption. They appraise their bodies, figures, wrinkles, "assets" coolly, with the intent to rectify or conceal what is wrong and accentuate what is right. They position themselves as heterosexual body objects, instead of body subjects, in the mating and dating market, searching for Mr. Right in much the same way their moms did when they were coming of age in the 1950s.

This is sometimes defended as postfeminist progress beyond the authoritarian and puritan 1960s feminism of the founders, who insisted on hairy legs and forbade makeup. The subtext here is homophobia, as Gen-X and Gen-Y women position themselves as straight, interpreting the subject positioning of erstwhile feminist bodies as, in effect, lesbian separatism. Younger women today are male identified, in Rita

Mae Brown's term, they welcome the male gaze and adorn and exercise themselves accordingly. In this context, to be thin is to be feminine, not the antique femininity of the Victorian era, which is unnecessarily corseted, but the hip femininity of "you can have it all": jobs, credit cards, a toned body, drooling men, even children.

The Body Subject and a Politics of Needs

Postfeminists have attempted to remove the body from politics, into which it was inserted by 1960s feminists, existential phenomenologists, early Marx, and the Freudian left—a diverse cast of body-theoretical characters! All of these have had trouble with the idea of Descartes's disembodied ego, who merely thinks. And Freud, Marx, and feminist theorists have all noticed that the body has become a contested terrain on which all sorts of depth-psychological, familial, sexual, and political skirmishes take place. To be sure, Frankfurt School–influenced theorist Russell Jacoby cautioned in *Social Amnesia* (1975) against a "politics of subjectivity" that reduces every political valence to the self, ignoring the powerfully colonizing forces of traditional politics and capitalist economics. The body subject is political, but not all politics involves bodies and selves. The body is especially political as capitalism has infiltrated the private sphere, including the body and psyche, with rapid information technologies tying us to discourses and practices that aren't good for us, such as buying on credit, eating high-fat foods, and plastic surgery. In a faster capitalism we recognize that the body, psyche, and self are even more plastic, more manipulable, than we realized before the Internet, television, and media culture. And capitalism must colonize bodies because its growth of markets must be intensive as well as extensive, not relying on global cultures of consumerism to keep it afloat. The body must be recruited, commodified, and objectified to keep people shopping and to divert

Eros, the life instincts, from what Marcuse (1955) identified as their drive to be free not of civilization but of deadly social forces (Thanatos).

Diet is a good example of all this. Fast capitalism persuades people to get in their cars and visit Taco Bell, which stays open late. They empty their pockets in doing so. But in desiring Taco Bell people are diverted from their real needs, which, as early Marx (1964) recognized, include meaningful work, community, and political liberty. This opens the question of false needs, a perennial headache for critical theory, which risks preaching and legislating, imposing values and needs from Apollonian heights. A careful reading of Marcuse's *One-Dimensional Man* (1964) suggests otherwise: He defines false needs as needs not freely determined but rather imposed, if subtly and subliminally, through advertising and the culture industries. People, when free, will use reason, the venerated Hegelian-Marxist capability, to determine what is best for them, their bodies, their families. Nowhere do early Marx and the Frankfurt School suggest that everyone will have the same particular needs—oatmeal, brown rice, sushi, smoothies—but they will share the need for political freedom and meaningful, noncoerced work. I would add to the Marxist and Frankfurt agendas the need for healthy bodies and families, a desideratum of feminists and greens who recognize the politics of selfhood, food, exercise, makeup, and clothing as a significant issue for twenty-first-century theorists and activists.

The body is especially an agenda item for a discussion of false, self-destructive needs at a time when the body is increasingly mobilized, quite contradictorily, to overeat fatty foods and then purchase diet pills and exercise equipment. This contradiction, which I noted earlier, lies at the heart of a body-political critical theory appropriate to a fast/fast-food/feasting/fasting capitalism. Underlying the politics of the gorging self is orality, the ways in which needs are compartmentalized so that they can be satisfied orally and not also genitally, "polymorphous perversely," as Freud termed it approvingly. The compartmentalization of desire is a hallmark of a capitalism that denies people meaningful work and nurturing community but otherwise satiates their endless desires piecemeal, through shopping, Internet surfing, and eating/dieting. Oral compulsions exist because people aren't truly fulfilled in the ensemble of their activities. The body subject is only an object, acted upon by media culture and various political economies that compartmentalize desire so that people can let off steam—Freud's desublimation.

In *Eros and Civilization* (1955), perhaps the earliest statement of the thesis of a fast capitalism, Marcuse argues that in post–World War II capitalism desublimation is almost always "repressive," giving people outlets that are both unhealthy and diverting. Their bodies become object, not subject, impacted by the food, diet, and exercise industries as they gratify themselves orally, not also polymorphously, in terms of the totality of their existence. What would be genuinely polymorphous today, in an accelerated capitalism? The self would experience its body as a unity of sense and sentience, its opening to the world and to other people. The body wouldn't be estranged from the person, as it frequently is when we are sick, overweight, stressed, and flabby. People wouldn't experience release only in sexual climax but would treat themselves and others sensuously, reveling in the experience of embodiment and of others' bodies. This would, of course, require the overthrow of puritanism, which, as Weber understood, was a prerequisite of capitalist development. I am not arguing against, or for, monogamy but suggesting that polymorphous liberation would not only liberate the body, and other bodies, but also sexualize/sensualize the culture in ways that render the debate over pornography moot.

Images of the body, and of sexual bodies, are deemed pornographic precisely because the body and desire are unfree today. Watching anonymous people have sex doesn't usually lead to violence against women, the overdrawn argument of the more puritanical wing of feminism; it simply makes the viewer want to have sex. Yet, as Marcuse argues, gratification must not be limited to oral or genital sexuality but must involve the whole person in her relation to herself, others, community, and nature. This would involve diet and one's relationship to animals and meat. Marcuse recognizes that there is a link between the body and nature, and thus between desire and history, that requires us to ground desire in the whole body subject and not simply in the erogenous zones, which are the primary focus of most pornography today. In a better society, sexuality/sensuality would involve the body in motion, the body farming and gardening, the body playing sports, the body lifting weights and working itself out, the body making love and reading about and watching others similarly engaged.

Pornography is the compartmentalization of desire, the objectification of the body and of bodies. Desire includes but isn't limited to sex. Eating can be sensual, as can playing tennis. After a morning in the gym lifting weights and then playing a couple of sets of tennis, followed by a low-fat lunch with my wife, I am aglow with the unity of sense and sentience, even if this fades as I fight through traffic in my town without public transportation and deal with other aspects of the damaged life, such as my children's ridiculous homework load and watching televised images of Iraqi children killed by American "smart" bombs. Pornography is puritans' name for the representation of sexuality, which, if transformed in a polymorphous political and economic order, could unlock desire not only to have orgasms but to change existence and the order of things (see MacKinnon 1988, 1993).

Sex isn't the only thing threatening the status quo. So are vegetarianism, atheism, hard-core exercise, radical ecology, reading and writing, contemplation and meditation. All of these disrupt what Marcuse terms the "performance principle" of puritanical productivism, which allows only occasional pornographic sexual release, binge eating, and vacations.

129

Productivism and performativity, to which pornography might be read as an inadequate response, are intensified in an accelerated Internet capitalism. More than ever body subjects must reinterpret desire as a constructive political agenda, theorizing the body as a battleground and taking steps to reclaim it from the culture industries.

6

Slowmodernity

I have argued that capitalism has quickened since World War II, especially with the advent of the Internet. People work harder and more; their private space has been eroded; kids are doing adultlike amounts of homework and activities; people eat badly, on the run, and then embark on crash diets and exercise programs. The world is ever-present and omnipresent, saturating us with stimuli, discourses, directives. It is difficult to gain distance from the everyday in order to appraise it. Our very identities as stable selves are at risk. We need to slow it all down.

TUNING IN, TURNING ON, DROPPING OUT

Slowing down is easier said than done. The self is so embattled, bombarded from all sides at all hours via all media, that reclaiming it, as if we ever had it in the first place, is a tall order. Heroic measures are usually futile. And yet the 1960s taught us, first in the antiwar and civil rights movements and then the women's movement, that the self matters. The self is political, as are everyday life, the body, food, sex, exercise, and culture—even if not all politics involves the personal, sexual, dietary, and cultural. Critical theory and postmodernism powerfully teach us that discourse, language, writing, media, cultures, bodies, and bedrooms are the new contested terrain of post–World War II, post-Fordist, fast and now faster capitalism. The forces of capital and control, those who benefit from disempowering selves, have colonized what used to be off limits to the social and political. They have done so, as I have been arguing, largely to find new markets and at the same time divert people from the revolutionary deed or, as Timothy Leary and hippies preferred during the sixties, from dropping out (and perhaps dropping acid). Marcuse (1955) said it well when he talked of the late-capitalist performance principle, according to which all life, experience, diet, sex, and leisure are mobilized in order to reproduce the existing order, denying a Dionysian desire that would recognize the prospect of liberation inscribed in advanced technologies capable of finally delivering us from scarcity. Performativity is the logic of faster capitalism, subjecting all of life, and even children's existence, to scheduling, producing, connecting, messaging, immersing oneself in the quotidian and therefore losing sight of the bigger picture.

This bigger picture, like a complicated jigsaw puzzle or mosaic, can only be grasped from the vantage of distance. Adorno (1978) and his Frankfurt colleagues identified distance as the vantage of critical reason, from which we can appraise our damaged lives, figuring out what bonds us and then what we can do to burst free. Marcuse argued that distance, and thus critical consciousness, was being reduced because in late capitalism people are so immersed in everyday life that they can't stand outside of it in order to appraise it. This is one of my main contentions about a fast and faster capitalism: People's lives are so accelerated that they cannot slow down sufficiently to take stock let alone begin to change things. It is all people can do to keep up with the frenzy of cyberspace—e-mail, cell phone calls, instant messaging, directives from the boss, children's frantic schedules, a substantial and growing workload that respects neither temporal nor physical boundaries.

Adorno chose the spatial metaphor of distance and closeness to characterize the predicament of the social critic who must work hard to separate himself from the everyday in order to gain a critical perspective on it. I choose the metaphor of time, passing rapidly or slowly, in order to suggest that social critics must slow down their worlds in order to grasp and then reorder them. We must turn off television and the cell phone; we must not obsess about our e-mail; we must insulate our children against an incipient, premature adulthood; we must slow down and think things through, carefully evaluating modernity for its strengths and weaknesses and not simply accepting existence as a plenitude of social being.

Although people in modern cultures are better educated than in Marx's time, Marx could gain the vantage of social criticism more easily than we can because the issues were more basic then—getting enough to eat, finding shelter, providing for one's family, escaping political tyranny. Today the issues seem more nuanced as we live amid abundance, if not for everyone. Let us not forget that one out of every four Americans lives near, or below, the poverty line, which is currently considered to be an annual income of $17,900 for a family of four. Try to buy groceries, pay rent, perhaps maintain a car, acquire health insurance, and even save modestly for future education on that pitiful sum. And without education one's children will be destined to relive one's own penury, locked into a cycle of poverty that seems natural, inescapable, for its tenacious hold on minds and bodies.

Barbara Ehrenreich (2001) documents the working poor who subsist at the margins of our economy and society, desperately clinging to the edge of subsistence while doing exhausting, degrading part-time jobs without benefits. But the lives about which Ehrenreich writes do not include her own, which affords her not only distance—and with it education, time, hope—but also the luxury of shedding her life and taking on another, "going underground" to experience firsthand what it's like to live as the working poor do. Ehrenreich does this as a literary methodology, a way of getting inside other selves more desperate than her own. But no matter how

133

bleak her lot while working at Wal-Mart or for a maid service, she always knew that she was "going home," out of penury and back to security, from the vantage of which she could engage in important social criticism. Ehrenreich masterfully combines distance and immersion in order to tell the stories of selves denied the privileges of time, food, housing, health care—stability.

For the poor and desperate, distance, and with it hope as well as systematic anger—expressed as theory—is unattainable and probably even unimaginable. For the comfortably college educated and middle class, distance, contemplation, and critical thought are rejected as a violation of utility and performativity. They are "good for nothing," a waste of time. As the vast majority of my students ask me and my colleagues, "Is it going to be on the test?" "Am I responsible for the lectures or the readings?" "Do I have to have footnotes?" "Exactly what pages do I have to read?" Some of my colleagues, in frustration, give objective tests, supposing that real understanding can be sacrificed for a modicum of content, given that most of our students are unmotivated, turned off by the intellectual life. They merely imitate their parents and the culture at large, which substitute performance for thought and utility for intrinsic value. The theoretical life won't pay the mortgage, car note, tuition, or credit card bill.

My argument risks being a romantic one for distance, contemplation, and quietude—life lived at a snail's pace in order to take stock and then take action. Our culture needs romanticism in order to arrive at the electric moment when thought becomes action, first on the personal level and then collectively, even globally. It also needs humanism, as I will explore later, at the risk of offending postmodernists who have given up on selves. We need to contemplate utopia and, implicitly, our distance from it, even as we acknowledge that fantasies often turn into nightmares if accompanied by hubris, arrogance. It takes dexterity, subtlety, and nuance to engage in social criticism and visionary theory without being prescriptive; our problems are common, but our solutions may vary with context, culture, race, gender, generation. Most visions end up being hallucinations, distorting and deceiving. And yet not to fantasize condemns one to the quotidian, to what I am calling immersion and instantaneity, which block distance, critique, and action. My students are utilitarian because the culture at large elevates performance and production over judgment and reflection. Again, this is the meaning of Marcuse's concept of one-dimensional thought.

Worldliness has become a plague, blunting critical insight by bending it back toward earth and not into outer space, with utopian reach. We are too worldly not only in the sense that we have too many experiences and know too much trivia but also in that our experiences rush by so quickly that we cannot pause to consider what is happening to us and why. Worldliness involves immersion and instantaneity, being swallowed up by things that, in themselves, are coveted, and living in the moment instead of considering many moments, both past and future. The present becomes eternal, devoid of history, which includes the possibility of a different, better future. The character trait best suited to this everyday world of instant, all-encompassing experience is versatility, the ability to adapt to whatever comes one's way, rapidly. We learn quickly, even as children, that we must be flexible, roll with the punches, compromise, accept what we cannot change. Of course, this acquiescence has always been taught by religion, which, as Marx knew, blunts critical consciousness and discourages utopia as well as revolution.

We begin to learn these lessons in school and in our early play groups (see Bowles and Gintis 1976). Many report cards have grades for "citizenship," which combines conformity and obedience. As kids we are also taught instrumental rationality, how to study for tests and turn in homework in order to earn good grades that will ease our way into comfortable adulthood. By the time we get to high school, many American kids already know what they want, which are essentially lives like their parents'—suburbia, white-collar jobs, vacations, cars, electronic technologies for entertainment and communication. Our needs have already been determined, indeed overdetermined, by peers, parents, and the media. It is already too late to become critical theorists, let alone political activists. Childhood and adolescence have rushed by, barely allowing kids pause to locate themselves in a world not of their making and to question the value of values, let alone ask the question of questions. It is for this reason that we must turn to childhood and schooling in order to slow down the virtual self.

Raising Different Kids

My kids are already different from their peers. They aren't yet allowed to stay home alone. They don't know much about cars or colleges. They don't have boyfriends or girlfriends. They don't have their own phone line or televisions in their rooms. They have traveled beyond North America, and they eat weird foreign food, but they aren't worldly in the sense of knowing what is on late-night television or the plots of the latest R-rated movies. We talk about sex and define scatological terms for them in order to sate their curiosity, but they aren't yet sexualized. They play instruments and sports, too, but not on "select" teams that require monthly fees, a contract, emotional intensity, and rigorous practice and travel schedules. They go to bed early by their classmates' standards, and they never stay up overnight in order to toilet-paper houses. Sometimes, they say they feel deprived by neighborhood and schoolroom standards, but we know better.

My wife and I are purposely slowing down our kids' lives where we can. Although they often have mountains of homework, we keep their schedules fairly clear so that they can decompress from the accelerated pace of school and of life. We want them to play, to rest, to explore, to think, to be kids. We know other parents who recognize that kids grow up too fast, and we encourage our kids to play with their kids and not with worldly, jaded kids. We put a premium on studiousness, but not on grades or test scores. As academics, we recognize that test taking is an art and that much homework, especially the taxonomic kind requiring mere memorization, adds little, if any, value (see Kralovec and Buell 2000). We want our kids to read and to want to read. We want them to be creative, writing stories and plays, which they enact. They go to theater camp in the summer and art classes during the year.

This combines a slowing down of life with enrichment, a delicate, but not impossible, balance. There is a difference between being worldly, in a superficial sense of knowing the "latest" cultural trends, and being firmly situated in the world and then being curious about it. We want our kids to ask questions, to interrogate authority and rules, to think critically and not accept what is given to them. We want them to be expressive and not passive or downtrodden. In the American South, including Texas, kids are often taught to call their elders "sir" or "ma'am." When I first heard this, I immediately read southern "manners" for the social-psychological underpinnings of authoritarianism, involving deference and idolatry. We are Yankees (a southern pejorative for states on the "wrong" side during the Civil War), and we want our kids to be Yankees! We also want them to be respectful. The challenge is to inculcate respectfulness while teaching children not to be submissive.

The challenge of raising kids, then, is to insulate them from the world while teaching them about the world. They need Adorno's precious quality of mind called distance, differentiating knowledge and the knower from the everyday in order to question its rightness and permanence. The key philosophical term here is *historicity*, a way of viewing the present, and facts, as grounded in the past, which bore them, and opening to a possible but not necessary future. Thus, one can analyze today's capitalist economy as stemming from feudalism and the beginnings of the Industrial Revolution and stretching into the immediate and perhaps even distant future. But the economy, like everything else in the world that bears the human imprint, is defined by "historicity." That is, just because we have known capitalism for over a century and know it today does not mean that it must endure forever, as non-Marxist social theorists such as Durkheim, Weber, and Parsons allege. History's final chapter has yet to be written.

We teach our kids to view the world through the lenses of historicity, recognizing "why" things are the way they are, rooted in the past, but at the same time recognizing that the social world is fluid and can be transformed. This transformation must pass through selves, people like you and me who inhere in everyday life and aren't oblivious to it and yet who grasp the big picture, necessarily known through paradigms and not simply through the accumulation of piecemeal evidence. After all, evidence is a text, a mode of rhetoric, argument for one state of affairs or another. Positivism is a text urging people to give in and give up, to accept the given instead of recognizing their own potential for "giving" it, and giving it differently.

This argument for (or perhaps, better, from) agency risks being another politics of subjectivity, issuing in self-improvement and individual attainment, all the way from better jobs to better bodies and better mates. Although the personal matters, as feminism has taught us, so does the political, which, in these postmodern times, positions the personal as its accomplice. False needs are imposed on the self and then internalized so that they appear to be one's own choices. But politics is not exhausted by the personal, even as it mobilizes everyday life, sexuality, bodies, desire, even the unconscious. It is all too easy for our children to hear our arguments from agency—"you can be anything you want to be"—as personal and not also political arguments, which in some cases they certainly are. Todd Gitlin (2003) recently published a book, sold tellingly in the self-help section at Barnes & Noble, offering advice to young radicals and activists. Gitlin wants the next generations to commit the revolutionary deed, but with gentle guidance and admonitions from ancient 1960s radicals such as him and me! When I first saw the book, I realized that Gitlin and I were, in parallel ways, addressing the post–baby boom generations who, we hope, can learn to connect personal and political agency.

SELF-CARE, ALTERNATIVE LIFESTYLES, COUNTERHEGEMONY

The weight of what anthropologists call culture bears down heavily on all of us, unless we live on a desert island. The movie *Castaway,* in which forsaken airline passenger Chuck Noland (played by Tom Hanks) is stranded on just such a desert island, showed how culture and the self were called into question in its depiction of Noland's struggles to stay alive and remain hopeful about his rescue. Noland had to create a modicum of civilization for himself, not just finding food and building shelter but also creating myths of meaning that revolved around his past life and his hope of regaining it by being found. He had little to sustain hope, apart from a picture of his wife that survived the airplane crash and a ball that he fashioned into a totem that he animated by giving it a name. He created his own culture, in solitary confinement on that distant island, and thus he saved himself, giving himself the psychic resources with which to embark on a desperate voyage home.

Even on this deserted island, Noland wasn't inured to the effects of culture. He brought with him both the material culture of his few remaining possessions and the ensemble of his ideal culture, including his values, impulses, priorities, and pragmatism—his theory, by another name. Culture—theory— saved him by giving him both hope and a game plan for escaping the island's lonely hold. Even the most isolated and forlorn among us, in prison or the mental prisons of our own making, can exercise Sartrean agency and change ourselves and even begin to change the world around us (see Sartre 1976). As Hegel and then existentialism demonstrated, consciousness can never be entirely imprinted by the edicts and structures, which often appear intractable, of the outer world (see Poster 1975). Marx seized on this insight and argued not for a solitary consciousness but for collective consciousness, of the proletariat, with which to uproot old orders and create new institutions.

Marx assumed that workers would communicate effectively with each other, beginning on the factory floor and in the everyday sites of their daily existence, about the evils of capitalism and how to overcome them in a new society. They would write and read pamphlets and theoretical treatises, opening themselves to political education that would overturn the falsehoods of bourgeois ideology. This ideology argues that the world cannot be changed and thus workers—everyone—must content themselves with their meager lot. People could hope for modest self-betterment, through savings and the acquisition of skills, but not for radical changes in social structures.

At stake in a faster capitalism is the status of consciousness and then communication. Marx did not foresee the extent to which people's minds and needs could fall prey to advertising and pro-capitalist political theories. He assumed a mode of consciousness that could distinguish between true and false claims and thus overthrow all ideologies. He assumed reason and rationality, where today they are very much at stake. He assumed the ability to engage in clear discourse and to achieve consensus. Fast capitalism, and its accelerated Internetworked version, has laid waste to reason and reasoning, requiring selves to escape the gravitational pull of the everyday in order to imagine, and work toward, different worlds.

The Internet is a literary vehicle, composed of and calling forth millions of literary and interpretive acts. One cannot find definitive answers if by that we mean we can find Web pages we can simply trust without questioning their authority and digging beneath their claims for what is left unsaid. Internet postings are no less literary, indeed fictional, than other literary versions. One finds contradictory, incomplete, question-begging, carping, purposely deceiving, and made-for-profit pages. This can be confusing for amateur surfers interested in finding out the truth of things, whether the cheapest airfare to Orlando or the best way to treat tennis elbow. The inherent ambiguity and indeterminacy of the Internet—of course, of all knowledge—is *undecidability,* by which Derrida means that sentences don't end other sentences but instead beget new ones, in questioning and clarification. Even science, as I and others have written often (Agger 1989b, 2000; Aronowitz 1988), is susceptible to a Derridian deconstruction, revealing science's text to be every bit as undecidable as a poem, novel, or music video.

This doesn't defeat self-education, and thus alternative lifestyles, via the Internet, in effect slowing down capitalism. It doesn't mean that we must be cynical about writings and, thus, all theoretical systems, as nihilist deconstructors sometimes are. Rather, the occasion of the Internet's inherent democracy and polyvocality should be seized on as an occasion for new texts and thus new worlds—new ways to live, work, raise families, become educated, get fit, and eat better. Today, the weight and speed of capitalism compel private solutions to our problems, for which we consult self-help pages and enter chat rooms devoted to single issues. But it is conceivable that Internet-based reading and writing can do more than change individual lives, instead shifting power and building community in ways that defy the commodifying, conformist tendencies of capitalism.

As long as we understand that the self's experiences are fundamentally social, stemming from overbearing social structures of work, family, education, leisure, and diet, we can deal with the self's problems as social problems. Eating more fish and less meat, working out regularly, finding jobs that don't require dishonesty and alienation, and decelerating the pace of children's lives and schooling can become not only personal adjustments—alternative lifestyles—but genuine modes of counterhegemony, by which I mean fighting capitalism and figuring out alternatives to it that have meaning and momentum (Gramsci 1971). This risks being heard as a timeworn utopianism, a long journey beginning with a single step. I remain convinced by feminists, existential Marxists, and the Frankfurt School that social change must change people—and requires people to be changed for it to occur, in the fateful simultaneity of self- and social change. What is so difficult today is imagining that self-change can occur so massively, globally, and rapidly that incremental changes cumulate into major structural transformations. And yet the Internet makes this easier to imagine than even 15 years ago, when I wrote *Fast Capitalism* (1989a), and certainly than 150 years ago, when Marx published *Capital* (1967, originally published in 1867). The Internet helps us imagine, and then exploit, the protean connection between selves and social structure as we enter others' worlds and affect them with quick keystrokes using DSL connections.

The Dialectic of Discourse: Decline or Democracy

As Garfinkel's (1967) ethnomethodology helps us understand, discourse constitutes social structure—the ways in which we talk about, and then resolve, social quandaries, such as how to make ourselves understood in a rapidly moving, complex, imperfect, noisy world. We find ways to "do" social structure—of families, work, schools—from the ground up, using our ingenuity, inferential abilities, empathy, and especially our literary skills, decoding what others and the media say and then communicating with others. Garfinkel helps us understand that underlying social structure are discourse, consensus, and sense making, not abstract social laws identified earlier by Parsons (1951) as the moving force of a sociological invisible hand. Parsons's lawlike "pattern variables" of adjustment, integration, boundary maintenance, and goal setting are fictions, just terms for what people ordinarily do as they read the paper in differentiating truth from fiction, help their kids with homework, finesse a micromanaging boss, or conduct themselves at neighborhood meetings. People "do" these things using their powers of discourse, inferring, interpolating, imagining, signifying—deconstructing, by another name.

The Internet is a sprawling, global, nearly instantaneous vehicle of discourse and, thus, of social structure. It is replacing newspapers, magazines, television, movie theaters, CD players, and even books. It is replacing pulp, which comes from trees. When I chaired a faculty job search in my department, we no longer wrote letters of acknowledgment to applicants or to their references. We used e-mail to do the search, saving on postage, stationery, and telephone bills. Using e-mail helps speed up the process of a faculty job search, which, in this case, is probably a good thing because we are helping candidates sort out their job-market options more efficiently. But replacing pulp in other respects is very problematic, preventing people from writing and receiving letters, which they peruse and savor, attending public theaters and concerts, and reading and writing books that matter. The Internet, a frictionless vehicle of discourse and thus of social structure and self-change, has the potential for enhancing democracy and overthrowing capitalism, which thwarts democracy, but, in its conformist, commodified version, accelerates what I have called the decline of discourse. Democratized discourse resists and reverses discourse's decline, yet again demonstrating that the Internet is dialectical, possessing the contradictory potential for liberation and domination.

It is tempting to call for a return to pulp as a panacea—an era of slow publishing, transportation, mail, journalism, entertainment, education. Here, pulp is a metaphor for considered

143

reflection, which takes time and requires distance from its object. But pulp can be a conservative metaphor where we return to a mandarin or high culture in which very few have the opportunity to write books, let alone wield political and economic power. It is a contemporary metaphor for the elite organization of academic social science, in which the opportunity to publish articles in refereed journals is restricted to a lucky few who sport the correct letterhead, have friends in high places, and use the quantitative methodologies prevailing in midwestern empiricism. Pulp, as counterpoint to the Internet, is also dialectical, requiring the distance and time necessary for critique or reinforcing elite codes of disciplinary and cultural power closed off to nearly everyone.

Imagine Adorno answering his e-mail or putting up a personal Web page! This is a credible image, given his interest in technologies of culture and art. I suspect that he would have been skeptical, as I am here, about digitality, in Negroponte's sense, as a panacea for personal and social problems, just as he would have rejected the technological utopianism of Daniel Bell's postindustrialism (which is a veiled attack on Marxism, from which Bell [1960] broke). And the Frankfurt School, writing for the most part before Garfinkel's ethnomethodology and French postmodern theory, did not place emphasis on discourse as a basis of social structure. They were more traditional Marxists who retained Marx's original nineteenth-century concept of ideology even as they addressed an accelerating capitalism of state intervention and the culture industries. But I can envision Adorno not only sending e-mails to Horkheimer, separated by their travels but also theorizing the Internet—pixels and/or pulp, decline and/or democracy—as a stage of faster capitalism in which we can no longer assume the separation of text and world (subject and object). Our inability to assume this separation would have led Adorno to address what I am calling the decline of discourse, but it might have led him, and it certainly would have led Marcuse (always more upbeat and engaged), to seize on the permeable

144

boundary between culture and society, critique and social structure, as an occasion for what Gramsci (1971) first called counterhegemony—critique and action bridging the self and structures within which selves are constituted.

This work has already begun as latter-day critical theorists such as Luke, Kellner, Poster, and I have addressed a virtual, postmodern, faster capitalism and its contradictory potentials for further decline or greater democracy. Inspired by the Frankfurt School but conditioned by television, music, and movies, we recognize that the decline of discourse occasioned by the Internet and media culture might reverse itself toward greater democracy, even undoing capitalism as we know it, if people learn to use information, communication, and entertainment technologies in order to live different lives and become different selves. It cannot be ignored that as I am writing these words, millions of people in the United States and abroad are not lying on their couches watching television while drinking beer but busily composing—themselves—on the Internet, even if few of them have read *Capital, Fast Capitalism, Screens of Power* (Luke 1989), *What's the Matter with the Internet?* (Poster 2001), or *Media Culture* (Kellner 1995). They are learning how to live better and they are creating community. It is easy to see the political potential of this discursive activity, which is, above all, literary work—reading, interpreting, writing, revising.

As capitalism speeds along, people use the Internet and other information technologies to connect to and organize their work, home, school, kids, friends, and leisure activities. As I have been arguing, this sucks people into hurried, unstudied lives immersed in the everyday. What I am trying to do here is not abandon everyday life but connect it to utopia. The casualty of capitalism's acceleration since the late 1980s has been reason, a word inimical to instrumental rationality and even to postmodernists, who fear dogmatic reason. But the Freudian Marxism of the Frankfurt School, especially Marcuse, the embodied existential Marxism of Sartre (1956) and

145

Merleau-Ponty (1964a, 1964b), and left-wing feminist theory demonstrate convincingly that one can develop reasons and rationalities that do not trample the self or defoliate nature. This embodied, humane reason was grounded in the body subject by early Marx, who begins critical theory, from which I draw here.

By partaking of the Internet's opportunities for busy textuality (both as readings and writings), people enticed to live the fast life can also slow it down by developing the capacity for discourse and thus citizenship, both understanding and mastering their everyday worlds. The Internet is a trap, but also a vehicle of practical reason and critique. Garfinkel, contrary to Parsons, helps us understand social structure as the contingent everyday practices of people situated in their life-worlds. People don't necessarily possess perfect information, advanced degrees, endless leisure, and ample resources. They cannot always understand or make themselves understood. Yet, as Garfinkel demonstrated, people create meaning out of chaos, becoming adept at a communicative competence that helps them make sense of indeterminacy, imperfect information, and misunderstandings as well as poverty, racism, and sexism. Garfinkel's self is similar to Sartre's efficacious agent of *Being and Nothingness* (1956), both of which derive from early Marx's self of praxis—he who imprints himself on the world through work and achieves communion with others and with nature.

The literary self isn't always already political but can become political as we write and read our way out of bad habits, unreflected rapid routines. I am not saying that chatting online is a paradigm, or embryo, of liberation but, rather, that chatting is an example of an embryonic textuality that models self-determination and communicative competence. This potential to do discourse, to write, read, and chat critically, can become political when oriented to building community and rearranging power. Garfinkel showed that everyday selves create social structure, which, by implication, they can transform using different political frameworks. His—and phenomenology's—point is that the constitution of social structure always begins from the ground of everyday life and is not simply foisted on people from above by the custodians of alleged social laws (of differentiation, stratification, modernization, and so on) promulgated by nineteenth- and early-twentieth-century positivist sociology. To ignore people's capacity for what Sartre called agency—authorship—is an act of bad faith, abandoning the constitution of social structure to others, who are experienced as dominant.

SLOWMODERNITY

The critique of fast, and even faster, capitalism, much like the critique of fast food (Petrini 2003; Schlosser 2001), risks returning to a supposed golden age of premodern rural life. The "slow food" movement is a case in point, although Petrini implies a critique of capitalist mass production in his argument for local cuisine savored over a glass of indigenous wine. Who can disagree with his critique of McDonald's, especially where he brandishes bowls of pasta in metaphorical opposition? Schlosser's critique of the economic, workplace, and health perils of fat-laden, meat-driven fast food is an important part of my perspective on capitalism's acceleration. However, in embracing slow food and slow life we risk regressing behind modernity, which, as Habermas argues, needs to be defended even if, as he also notes, modernity's project has yet to be fulfilled. At issue here are metaphors of modernity and the implications they bear for a critique of a faster capitalism heavily reliant on the Internet and other social technologies of acceleration and globalization.

The speedup of social technologies and everyday lives breaks down important barriers between public and private required for people to engage in self-reflection and communication. People lose the vantage from which critique is possible.

This has always been the argument of the Frankfurt School. In my book *Fast Capitalism* (1989a), I revised Marcuse's critique of the eclipse of reason by noticing that capitalism has sped up, under sway of further Taylorism and Fordism, threatening the very status of the book as a vehicle of critique and persuasion. Today, things have gotten more perilous for critical reason because the Internet and other information and social technologies such as the cell phone and courier services make it even harder to gain the distance and time necessary for reflection and reason. The Internet and media cultures not only cause the book to decline further but also enable the penetration and colonization of everyday life, of consciousness itself. The wired world tempts us to abandon not only books in the traditional sense of texts that stand apart and require us to work at their meanings but all quiet time—here, the metaphor of slow life—during which we are not "connected."

The average American child spends five and a half hours a day using information and entertainment technologies, from television (by now a traditional medium) to computers and video games. This attenuates childhood and negates other developmental activities such as playing outside with other kids, reading, studying, and practicing music. The health risks are abundant as children who surf also gorge themselves on fatty fast foods and convenience foods. It seems obvious that the solution is to turn off the television and computer, to send kids out to play, and to return to family dinners with meals prepared from scratch.

The metaphor of slow life is appealing, but it risks an antitechnology posture that regresses behind modernity to a premodern pastoralism. Petrini sometimes implies that the good society would be a wine-tasting circle or dining club. Although I share his critique not only of fast food but also of fast life, requiring standardization, mass production, and globalization, the pastoral, almost premodern, alternative is fundamentally bourgeois; it would change very little, except for

Yuppies able to travel and savor regional wines and goat cheese (or, while they are at home, to shop and eat with a cosmopolitan sensibility). The problem, as Marx always recognized, is not technology but its uses. It is not the machine or factory system, or now the Internet, but the social contexts in which these technologies are deployed. At issue, as it was for Marx, is power, and notably the power accruing to wealth.

Postmodern critiques of the modern tend to focus on industry, factories, technology, science, and the loss of meaning (see Davis 1990; Harvey 1989; Soja 1989). These are compelling issues, but they can be better addressed within a modernist critique of modernity—Marxism. This is because Marx had no illusions about the superiority of the capitalist-modern over its premodern predecessors. Who doesn't prefer electricity over candlelight, hospitals over hospices, public schools over homeschooling? The upper-middle-class take these amenities for granted, which is why they can embrace "slow food" defined as regional cuisine and wine whose prices are prohibitive. Marx was a modernist, but he argued that capitalism doesn't exhaust modernity; indeed, it is the penultimate stage of prehistory, after which real history, modernity, can blossom, harnessing technology to human needs and pacifying our relationship to nature.

Slow food and slow life are important goals, but they must be situated within, and not before or beyond, modernity. I term *slowmodernity* a stage of civilization in which modernist manufacturing and information technologies are utilized to decelerate the pace of existence, thus redrawing the boundaries between private and public, self and society, that an accelerated postmodern/Internet capitalism has nearly dissolved. Petrini is correct to oppose agribusiness, pesticides, Taylorized fast-food restaurants, and supermarket chains in the name of slow life, but we must insert slowness into modernity in such a way that we don't eliminate certain fast technologies, including media culture and the Internet, that enable a literary democracy of the kind I have been describing. The slow must coexist with the fast—the modern—as we formulate a new vision of the end of history, which is neither the fast modernity of capitalism nor a postmodernity that abandons the project of modernity altogether. I side with Habermas (and Marx) on the value of modernity; I side with Derrida and Adorno on the hidden arrogance and dominance of a version of modernity springing from the Enlightenment; I side with Petrini on the superiority of penne pasta lightly tossed with olive oil and Parmesan or doused with marinara over the Big Mac. Together, these theoretical, existential, and culinary tendencies define what I am calling the slowmodern, a society as yet unfolding in which fast technologies, providing for basic needs and making electronic democracy possible, coexist with slower technologies of pulp books and old-fashioned letters, family dinners, long walks, and unencumbered childhoods.

The dilemma of the "slowing down" metaphor is that it risks Luddism, regressing to a premodern past. A technological utopianism based on speed fails to extricate capitalism, which pits speed against thought and text, from modernity, which has yet to be fulfilled. A modernity that remains capitalist, even using the Internet, thwarts Marx's projection of a society in which technology could be used to master nature in fulfilling human needs, allowing people time for praxis—self-creative work on a pacified nature. *Modernity as an image of the end of history needs to be transformed into slowmodernity, a final stage in which frictionless community building and literary work via the Internet and other informational and entertainment technologies coexist with the simple pleasures of slow life, slow food, slow bodies, slow families, and slow work.*

The issue, thus, isn't only pace or speed. In slowmodernity, the fast and slow coexist: People enjoy the slow life amid rapid cybercommunications and instant technologies that free them from scarcity (see Dyer-Witheford 1999). The issue, rather, is the ways in which fast technologies break down boundaries and barriers that used to insulate the self, and reason, against a forbidding outside world. As critical theory, deconstruction, feminism, and psychoanalysis all demonstrate, there is neither an unsullied "inside" nor impinging "outside" that is not somehow implicated in the other. The self, and its critical reason, was never a world apart, nor can it ever be, given its saturation with the social. And, as Marx demonstrated, we can create an "outside"—economy and culture—that doesn't thwart reason but instead embodies it.

Slowmodernity involves restoring certain boundaries, including those between public and private, self and society, text and world, and reason and its object. It also involves breaking down other boundaries, such as those between friends, neighbors, colleagues, and cultures. In a supposedly global era, ethnocentrism is arguably the greatest barrier to completing the project of modernity. The premodern threatens to undo culture and civilization, even as they bear the scars of inhumanity.

Retreat behind a boundary restores the self, who can dine, love, and exercise *slowly,* without time compression and acceleration. But one can also venture forth into the world, with minimal resistance, embracing globality, universality, and totality especially via the electronic prostheses that deprivatize the self. In fast capitalism, the self has the worst of both worlds: He is dominated in public by fast work, fast food, fast cars, even fast diets—fasting. This is the intensely social, saturated self (Gergen 2000) that cannot resist its constitution by, and as, the social object. And yet the self is denied a healthy and communitarian—no, communist!—privacy that includes the moment of publicity—friends, family, even colleagues. The person feels very much alone when the public/private boundary is assailed by media culture and the Internet, cut off from meaningful relationships, including, as Petrini reminds us, the experience of convivial dining.

In slowmodernity, people could live as quickly or slowly as they like, traveling far to sample regional cuisines and cultures or staying home to compose letters, read newspapers and books, author the culture—and themselves. Authorship is citizenship in slowmodernity, which combines the project of modernity—industrial production, democracy, cities, medicine, and science—with certain valuable premodern elements such as community, intimacy, ceremony, low-fat diets of organic, unprocessed food, exercise and physical exertion, papyrus and then pulp. The premodern is not to be condemned simply because mythology and dogma prevailed. There were important premodern counterforces that humanized agrarian Europe, affording what Weber called "enchantment" (1978). The subsequent disenchantment of the world by science, technology, industry, and globality eliminated these premodern vestiges that could have saved the project of modernity, notably capitalism, from itself, indeed from its pace and its destruction of boundaries, including the boundary between the self and world.

Although postmodern theory affords invaluable insight into the power and opportunities of discourse, revealing apparently nondiscursive accounts such as science to be decisive, deliberate authorial choices (that could have been made differently), the metaphor of the postmodern—"after" modernity—abandons slow life in favor of an informatic instantaneity. Fast life is assumed as either late-modern or genuinely postmodern, and utopia is depicted, by nonleftist postmodernists, as "life on the screen," not as life with others. But slowing things down can be formulated as a postmodern agenda if by postmodernity we understand the fulfillment of modernity's promise once modernity is no longer allowed to assail all boundaries.

This is another way of saying that fast and slow life—lives—can coexist, distinguishing between what is worthy about a modernity inextricably bound up with capitalism—medicine, health care, democracy, science, transportation, material and information technologies—and the premodern, which includes low-fat diets, conviviality, community. Indeed, this communitarian, agrarian premodern, less anchored in reality than in a Luddite, pastoral mythology of yesteryear before the machine

152

age, *transforms* the modern by shattering its capitalist framework. As he well understands, Petrini's argument for slow
food and slow life amounts to nothing if it does not destroy
agribusiness, slaughterhouses, supermarket chains, food and
lifestyle advertising, and the exploitation of minimum-wage
labor. It is harmless, even conformist, to suppose that one can
change the world by boiling one's penne pasta, sprinkling
aged cheese over it, and washing it down with a regional
wine. That changes nothing if it remains lifestyle, enjoyed by
a few while the rest are locked into alienated labor, fast lives,
fatty food, obesity, and meaninglessness.

The argument for a slowmodernity, thus, breaks from capitalism without abandoning the project of modernity. It borrows a premodern imaginary of slow life that it then blends
with fast-paced information, communication, and material technologies, freeing people from what early Marx called alienation. Images of slow life from premodernity help us disentangle
modernity and capitalism, issuing in a slowmodernity that can
be viewed as a desirable utopian endpoint. The slow purges
the fast of its boundary-shattering tendencies, instead allowing
people to rebuild boundaries and blend slow with fast in
ways that facilitate human needs—precisely Petrini's image of
slow life, as I understand it. It is remarkable that his imagery
of a slow life and slow food, which refreshes critical theory at
a time of impasse, comes not from communication theory
(Habermas 1984, 1987b) or aesthetic theory (Adorno 1984)
but from *food theory*. I found Petrini's book in the cooking
section of an Austin bookstore!

Food theory becomes critical social theory where we allow
diet and shopping to illuminate key issues of the public/
private relationship, global markets, and the body. I am inserting the argument for slow food and slow life into the discussion of modernity and postmodernity. I conceptualize the
completion of the project of modernity using images from
both the premodern and capitalist-modern (slow and fast,
respectively), issuing in a notion of slowmodernity that doubles

153

back on capitalist alienation and boundary shattering in order to return to a perhaps mythic notion of slow food, slow life, and slow community. In this light, we find the premodern inadequate because it is penurious and irrational; we find the modern inadequate because it is bound up with capitalism's conquest of nature and otherness; we find the postmodern inadequate because it disqualifies utopia. We retain from the premodern the notion of slow life, from modernity a promise of technological abundance and electronic democracy and community, and from the postmodern a questioning about the Enlightenment's dubious equation of reason and science.

All of this is to suggest, with Petrini, the Frankfurt School, and various leftist postmodernists and feminists, that progress needs to be reconceived not as conquest *of* but productive harmony *with* nature. Adorno viewed the desired end of history as the redemption of nature, which reflected his Nietzschean critique of the Enlightenment's Promethean will to power. Nature has its seasons and rhythms, to which all things return. Alienation from nature, especially in urban life and via interstate highways and expressways, takes its toll on the slow life, which needs to measure itself against nature's cycles of eternal recurrence. In slowmodernity, we will restore and redeem nature as a standard by which other activities and arrangements are judged. This is why food theory opens the way to a broader understanding of society and culture: Food is nature, and it reveals to us our own nature as sentient beings. The early Marx, Marcuse in his Freudian Marxism, feminist theorists of the body subject, and now Petrini help us theorize the body in nature, especially via food, diet, and exercise.

This is not puritanism, preaching abstinence, as Petrini indicates. One can revel in the reproduction of one's body through eating, especially, I would add, if one works the body hard, in both vocation and recreation. The spent body, toned and purged of the poisons of fast life, relishes cuisine and the conviviality of dining. Since most of us don't work with our hands and bodies, we require exercise—preferably sport—in order to be fit. But it is not only good health I am urging here; it is the experience of oneness with nature that comes from experiencing our bodies as both body subjects and objects, at once humanity and nature. Sartre and Merleau-Ponty well understood that existence is embodied, helping their existentialism move considerably beyond Descartes's thinking subject. I add here that the subject is also an eating and exercising subject, and a loving subject, that experiences full humanity when working on itself and replenishing itself with the fruits of slow life, cooked and eaten slowly, in sync with nature.

From Food Theory to Critical Theory, Body Politics to the Body Politic

In his argument for slow food and slow life, Petrini gives the impression that we can change the world by choosing a different restaurant, an *osteria* or small, independent establishment specializing in local cuisines and devoted to gourmets and gourmands. Or one might imagine that by turning off the television, unplugging the alarm clock, abandoning the cell phone, and going to the gym we can overturn established political power. These are but beginnings. The limitation of food theory and a body politics is that they tend to lack a firm foundation in critical social theory that links bodies to the body politic, even though they illuminate crucial ways in which we are dominated by food production, diets, lethargy, compulsive working—fast life generally. The opening of food theory to critical theory, of Petrini to the Frankfurt School, is the concept of boundaries, vital to good life but at risk when the body has been colonized and accelerated by injurious external forces.

I have argued that fast capitalism dismantles boundaries shielding the self, its critical reason, and even its body from the impinging world. Information, entertainment, and communication technologies tether the person to the world and make it nearly impossible to stand apart and gain distance necessary in order to think and then act. Although sometimes physical and involving space, boundaries are largely temporal, either insulating us or exposing us to a 24/7 world that streams through us and binds us to it. Food theory joins feminist theories of the body and existential perspectives on embodiment in illuminating the ways in which everyday bodies are damaged by a world that bursts through boundaries: We eat unhealthful prepared foods; we use expensive and self-objectifying cosmetics; we cannot escape the Internet and cell phones; stress and fatigue are chronic.

It is not enough, however, to illuminate the damaged self in a world without adequate boundaries. One must not only shield the self but also remake the world *through* the self, who, in slowmodernity, makes better choices, models good choices for others, and begins to build community and thus transform social institutions of culture, work, home, school, food, exercise, and bodies. Adorno, in exploring the extent to which the self has been damaged and reason eclipsed, draws attention to the public sphere's domination of private experience and existence. Accordingly, he wants to shield the self against what the Frankfurt School called domination. This is laudable and necessary. But, to shift metaphors, it is not enough for the person to choose pasta and exercise over fast food and lethargy. One must extend transformed existence into social change, a rebuilt public sphere that no longer stands against the person as controlling and external forces. Once boundaries are protected sufficiently to harbor and nurture the self, the self must then move outward and live— slowly and quickly at once—among others who become partners in what I am calling slowmodernity.

We thus go beyond the Frankfurt School's theme of domination to an existential, Marcusean, and feminist theme of transformation, not only undoing the public sphere's hold over privacy but also allowing the private to become public in its own right. Utopia begins at home. Indeed, what counts as "home" is no longer the same as for earlier generations and centuries, in which the barrier between private and public was clear and relatively impermeable. Home is now work, and work curiously homelike in its intimate collegiality. Both venues are open to the world, often too open, allowing the tentacles of discipline to choke off individuality and reason.

Struggling toward slowmodernity requires us to reboundary and deboundary our worlds at once, acknowledging that public and private, outside and inside, are now thoroughly implicated in each other. This insight is the bridge between food theory and critical theory, which swallows food theory whole, both preserving and extending its alimentary insights into the importance of body politics for the body politic. What should life be like in this, a new century? Let me offer an agenda, if not the only possible one.

1. *Periodically shut down the electronic prostheses dictating our worlds and lives.* If we must use them—think of the Internet—we should be selective and pragmatic, not allowing the possibility of connection to become an occasion for checking compulsively to see if we are connected. Shut off the cell phone; ignore e-mail; disable the answering machine and caller ID. Watch an hour of television, or less, unless television is crucial, such as during 9/11 or the Iraq war. If television must be watched, watch it with your kids so that you enjoy their worlds and help explain yours to them.

2. *Don't let home become a job or be overwhelmed by the job.* Set priorities that minimize work—time spent away from family, friends, personal projects. Nearly nothing we do in the way of paid work will have lasting impact. Articles and books published by academics over fifty take time away from avocations, family, children, the community. It is okay to work, and even necessary, but workaholism drowns the spirit. Don't

leave your kids in after-school care, or by themselves, unless you absolutely have to. Don't obsess about leaving work early, lest you miss an "important" meeting. All meetings are useless, by definition. And sucking up to the boss is inauthentic and ephemeral; bosses change, and you have to start all over again. Marx shrewdly recognized that zero work was to be the goal of his utopia. He also said that in a good society people would pick and choose among jobs that express themselves; they would become artisans again, and craftspeople. This includes writing, my chosen field.

3. *Eat healthful foods, both carbohydrates and proteins, preferably purchased from organic sources. Defy the supermarket chains and advertising for fast food and prepared food. Become athletes as a way of toning the body, restoring joie de vivre, overcoming depression and lassitude.* Athletes know what to eat; their bodies tell them: we need broccoli, rice, beans, some chicken. Athleticism overcomes alienation, as George Sheehan wrote in his inspiring *Running and Being* (1978), a meditation on the 1970s running boom (also see Rodgers 1980 on marathoning). You don't have to run, or even to like broccoli. But achieving a oneness with the body, what early Marx called the organic body, allows one to become intimate with nature and thus to destress. One sleeps better, dreams better, loves and lives better, feels stronger and more vital when one eats healthfully and exercises. The goal in this is not the body beautiful, if that means anorexia. The beautiful body is the body with which you feel at one. It is tireless, energetic, self-confident. And it dictates its own diet, which combines carbs (for energy) and protein (for the restoration of muscles). Fast fad diets are fake. They are tailored to people who don't exercise. Athletes know that you cannot eat only or mainly meat, as the Atkins diet counsels. Without carbohydrates as fuel, fatigue defeats the will to exercise. We must break out of the feast/fast dynamic in order to experience our bodies as vehicles of our humanity and our opening to nature.

4. *Don't overschedule—oneself or one's kids*. People have insufficient time for relaxation and avocation, let alone contemplation. As wealth increases (although not for everyone), time compresses and becomes scarcer. This should be no surprise, given the logic of capitalism: time is money precisely because it is through labor time that labor power transfers value to commodities and, hence, makes way for profit. Only the poor have time on their hands, too much time, given their unemployment or underemployment. But those who are above the poverty line need to reassess their exhaustive and exhausting commitment to paid work, shaving away hours that could be spent in more fulfilling ways than composing memoranda, typing e-mails, or networking. Few jobs afford flexible time, but this is exactly what people need in order to make good choices about vocation and career, trading time for money at the margin. School teachers enjoy the summer off, but few can afford to drive Lexuses. They are the richer for all that because they can travel, read, write, work out.

One needs time in order to be human. One also needs much of this time to be unstructured, not necessarily time for which one has planned. Well-managed selves "build" time into their hectic lives, for example reserving two hours on Thursday afternoons (barring office emergencies) "for themselves." Although those two hours are better than nothing, one needs *unplanned* time in order to enjoy the serendipity of real recreation and avocation—the time during which people discover themselves, often in surprising ways. I appear idle much of the time, reveling in the unplanned time of the academic leisure class. During this time, I think, play, work, and enjoy sociability with family and friends. It is a hallmark of our late-capitalist productivism and early-capitalist puritanism that we view such idle hours as purely "personal" time and not also time that is productive in the sense that it produces selves if not commodities.

5. *Defy productivism—use time to produce not commodities for market but selves for civil society and for family*. Viewed

this way, the self is a creation and a self-creation, precisely the sensibility early Marx (1964) discussed in his veneration of "praxis," self-creative and productive activity. The production and self-production of the self displaces and then altogether replaces commodity production as a societal goal. This assumes not necessarily high technology (complete automation and the total elimination of human toil) but *high-enough technology,* a central feature of slowmodernity as I intend it. This borrows from E. F. Schumacher's (1973) notion of appropriate technologies that spring from local cultures and levels of development. Sometimes, with Petrini, these can be "slow" technologies, whereas there can also be "fast" technologies, tending toward the elimination of human work altogether. The point is that we replace commodity production with self and community building as economic and societal goals, fundamentally displacing the value systems of Western societies.

6. *Actively work to transform our education systems, which should deal with "a mind at a time" (Levine 2002) instead of promoting a mass-production model of education for which there is a single fixed curriculum and accompanying standardized tests.* Mass-market education and standardized testing reflect a one-size-fits-all attitude toward education, and they betray a Fordist approach to schooling and curriculum. This is counterproductive even within a postmodern, post-Fordist capitalism let alone a postcapitalist society. Fordist education produces standardized students as commodities, using the assembly line as both metaphor and reality. In a post-Fordism edging toward slowmodernity, we must uncouple education and production, no longer educating young people "for" the workplace but helping them develop selfhood— identity, by another name. I tell my students that college, in addition to being about future vocation, is a time during which they can learn to be free and learn who they "are," also acknowledging that they can change who they are. They can learn to be free of assembly-line expectations, of confining

social norms, of the quotidian. They can learn to take intellectual risks, to think outside the box, to question and criticize.

Levine's notion of a mind at a time is a critique of a
standardized curriculum that ignores children with certain learning disabilities, such as Attention Deficit Disorder (ADD). Indeed, ADD, as a symptom of childhood distraction in the
busy classroom, is an outcome of an accelerated world in
which it is difficult for almost everyone to focus, given the
many, and rapid, stimuli bombarding us. The ADD child is the
accelerated child; indeed, ADD can be viewed as the mind's
and body's protest against the speed up, a way of disengaging
from the harmful, hurtful world of a fast-paced, fill-in-the-box
approach to education. Levine insists that kids diagnosed with
ADD are often the more creative ones, able to think outside
the box but not to do well on timed standardized tests. High
test scores and grades might actually signal intellectual dull-
ness and rigidity.

7. *Return to a view of the life cycle and childhood development that prolongs the preadult phases and shields kids from
the intrusion and acceleration of adulthood.* Removing productivism from education is not enough to liberate children.
We must take additional steps to reverse the abbreviation of
childhood in slowmodernity. Kids not only have too much
unimaginative homework, designed both to prepare them for
a Fordist workforce and to occupy their time, but also too
many other activities designed by parents and educators to
position them advantageously for college admission. And kids
know too much about adult topics such as sexuality, crime,
violence, shopping, brands, and professional sports. In some
measure, the attenuation of childhood reflects the privatization of children, who no longer fill their after-school hours
with aimless neighborhood play but have their hours structured for them by parents, teachers, coaches, and activity
mentors. We need to remove *structure* from childhood, which,
by definition, defies structuring and needs to be shielded from

structure so that kids can learn, acquire, and construct their identities using an approach that Kant called "purposively purposeless."

This involves both time compression and work expectations. Children need guidance and structure, to be sure, but they also need serendipity, which is one of the hallmarks of slow life in slowmodernity. They need unstructured play, and they need opportunities for creativity in school. My son learns more from voracious reading and from writing his own "books" than he does from most worksheets with blanks that are supposed to be filled in with a single correct answer. My daughter derives more benefit from writing and staging a play with friends than from her literature class, in which she must try to remember (in case of a quiz) what happened to a marginal character in chapter 2 after she has read ahead in the book. The underlying issue here is structure, and kids' need to be free of it regularly. Time and work/homework combine to thwart serendipity, which is the joyful and often mercurial process of finding and creating a self.

8. *Deprogram your kids from being overly concerned with their futures, and with success*—and this from a faculty member who values academic accomplishment! The attenuation of childhood involves shortening the life cycle of kids so that they must view virtually all K–12 activities, inside and outside the classroom, as "counting" toward college admission and thus successful adulthood. Very few things really count, as long as the child learns fairly normally, not falling behind. Indeed, what matters are not the traditional markers of academic success, from grades and test scores to extracurricular activities, but the opportunities kids need to discover what they like and are good at and then to pursue these activities and avenues. Not everyone has a knack or taste for geometry, or grammar, or public speaking, or shooting baskets. Emphasizing "everything" courts the child's disinterest in things she feels are being thrust on her by parents and academic author-

ities. This is not an elitist argument against mediocrity but simply an observation that kids need to discover their calling, which is tantamount to discovering what they are potentially good at, acknowledging, of course, that becoming good at something, whether the viola or computer science, requires a lot of hard but fulfilling work. Today, a lot of kids work hard, to the point of mental exhaustion, but they are intellectually lazy because their hard work doesn't answer to their muse.

I am not arguing against all childhood work, only against compulsive homework and resume building. I am in favor of hard work where it allows the child to become good at something, excelling, and where the child enjoys the work, the practice, for its own sake, a crucial lesson for adulthood. I am against career building where it substitutes for, and obstructs, building a life and a self—the real challenge for all of us. An instrumental rationality, whereby every activity is designed to meet a goal, defeats the purpose of childhood, which is to discover different rationalities, sensibilities, ways of living and relating.

9. *View and enact our everyday lives as always already political, not as irrelevant to, or beneath, politics.* I have struggled, as we all must today, with the multiple levels of self. In order to bring about social change, we must change ourselves; but we cannot change ourselves without promoting changes in others and in our institutions. At stake for this personal/public politics is time—how we spend our brief passage on earth, not hurriedly but with heart. Faster capitalism involves a certain production of time, which must be opposed. The overriding argument of this book is that we must reboundary the self, slow down our lives, and conceptualize and enact social changes that will take us to a higher level of modernity—slowmodernity. This level is not a Luddite retreat (slow), nor a digitized, cybernetic utopia (fast). It involves going back and moving forward, mastering time so that

163

it serves us and not the other way around. In *Being and Time* (1962), in which Heidegger launched existentialism just four years after Lukács founded Western Marxism in *History and Class Consciousness* (1971), Heidegger argued that the greatest existential problem is for people to accept their mortality. Once this was accomplished, people could live meaningful, authentic lives, making everyday choices that define them. Time does not defeat the human project, on this account, but enriches it, much as Marcuse transformed the so-called death instinct into an impulse to overcome alienation.

As the Frankfurt School understood, alienation involves forgetting—losing contact with the damaged lives that made this world possible. These lives, haunted by Gordon's (1997) ghosts, are being expended today, around the world and at home, and they were expended for most of human history, as travel to Mayan ruins, Cambodian killing fields, and the Holocaust's crematoria demonstrate. We are taught to forget so that we remain on task. Time is compressed into an eternal present so that we forget what brought us here. It is also compressed so that we extrapolate the present as we know it—malls, highways, schools, bodies—into an infinite future, forgetting the possibility of utopia, of radical rupture with the past and present. Time is at stake in the way we imagine ourselves as caught up in the contemporary, which is a postmodern form of consciousness. Immersion in the everyday isn't necessarily a truer form of experience, a phenomenological bracketing of the inessential, especially where everyday life is simulated by advertisers and ideologists in order to elicit it from consumer/ workers overwhelmed by working, spending, eating, and schooling.

Time is cluttered precisely so that we won't spend time pursuing the past and imagining a different future. As Weber understood, capitalism emerged from the Protestant Reformation, which placed value on busyness as well as business. In this book, I have addressed the production of time—its framings by dominant institutions and the selves who sustain them—

using categories such as Fordism, post-Fordism, fast capitalism, and faster capitalism. In effect, this is to deploy Marx's
central categories in ways appropriate to a late capitalism in
which economic exploitation and alienation become intensive
as well as extensive. It is not enough for people to work and
spend within nineteenth-century parameters of officially boundaried institutions, such as employment, family, leisure, religion. They can't produce and consume enough to sustain
capitalism. Global capitalism finds new markets and new producers, but that is only a partial solution. People in first-world
capitalist countries must also be accelerated through the colonization of their lifeworlds, to use Habermas's turn of phrase.

We must break the clocks, resisting and refusing the quickening of our lives. This is political protest and reconstruction
where it emerges from a theoretical understanding of faster
capitalism. We must not allow ourselves to be overscheduled,
hurried, hassled; we must take our sweet time, dawdling in
order to slow down the flow. This was well understood by
Walter Benjamin (1999) as he theorized the *flaneur,* who
strolled through Paris in order to drink deeply of cosmopolitan urban life as a mode of enjoyment, of existential being.
We must treat every day as a holiday, reading the newspaper
slowly, lingering over coffee, thinking through our plans, and
being flexible enough to change them as circumstances and
opportunities dictate. The flaneur is the antonym of the postmodern self who can multitask, juggle time and projects, pri-
oritize, set agendas, and work the room. The postmodern
business/busyness self dresses carefully, posturing the body
as commodity, whereas the flaneur recognizes that identity
lies deeper than mere appearances. Above all, wear an inexpensive, expendable watch that you can fling aside when it
becomes too confining.

10. *Refuse a disengaged social science, reject positivism and
a postpolitical postmodernism, and insert theory into practice.
We must embrace a leftist humanism—again.* The self who

initiates social change from within everyday life, recognizing that History is made body by body, family by family, workplace by workplace, must think theoretically, conceptually, about society and selves. Theory is understood here as generalizing activity, rising above the particular without sacrificing particulars—selves—to a transhistorical Reason or other abstractions that elevate liberty above lives. But theory is not a contemplative posture, or value free, as Marx and Engels understood in the last of their Theses on Feuerbach (1947). By the early twenty-first century, both positivism (midwestern-empiricist journal science) and postmodernism (Lyotard 1984; Rorty 1997) condemn politics either as bias or as authoritarian, grand theory having become grandiose. In our postpolitical age, what Jacoby (1975) called the politics of subjectivity reemerges as a studied posture, for example in postmodernism and postfeminism, both of which reject Marx and Engels's eleventh thesis on Feuerbach. This responds to the identity of political and personal, at the expense of the person, with a rejection of politics. Instead, as I have been arguing, the political and personal must be reboundaried without failing to understand their interpenetration; Adorno called that nonidentity. The personal is political, but not entirely, just as politics extends beyond family, home, and body.

Postpolitical quietism is tempting in faster capitalism, especially where official political institutions are hollow; think of the Supreme Court, the presidency, the Politburo. But politics can be reframed in slowmodernity as the simultaneous identity and nonidentity of public and private. This neither sacrifices bodies to a millenarian conception of progress, as we have done for over two thousand years, nor fails to recognize that our jobs, families, children, schools, diets, and bodies have fallen under the spell of what the Frankfurt School, following Weber, called administration. That politics has colonized the lifeworld—cultures, jobs, families, schools, bodies—doesn't mean we must withdraw from politics. Instead, we must reconfigure the polity and public sphere in a way that makes the self (see Bay 1958) the measure of all things, neither violating the self's ultimate interiority nor avoiding the self's responsibility to enter regularly the public sphere as a transforming and contributing agent.

Total administration or domination has deboundaried the self in relation to the public sphere, which is experienced as threatening or irrelevant. As such, the self must be reboundaried lest it simply dissolve, deconstruct, into nothingness. But the self's reboundarying should be matched by a deboundarying of private and public, person and politics, so that we recognize and act upon the inherence of politics in everyday life, again making man and woman the measure of all things. Petrini is absolutely correct that how and what we eat are political acts and have impact on the public sphere; the *osteria* always trumps the fast-food franchise as a locus and paradigm of humanity or what I am calling slowmodernity. If this is humanism, so much the worse for anti- or posthumanist philosophies of history, whether Althusserian (history without a subject) or postmodern (self merely as subject position). This humanism is the humanism of early Marx, who would have joined Petrini in fighting fast-food capitalism by brandishing bowls of penne pasta in protest.

Postmodern cynicism and irony are not adequate postures. Nor is liberalism, which dissolves the crushing weight of social structures into good intentions and rational choice. Don't be ashamed to be political, humanist, activist, Marxist, feminist. Embrace the eleventh thesis and oppose positivism. So much of who I am, and what I say here, is owed to the New Left, which stressed that change must pass through the self and everyday life (see Hayden 1962 and Miller 1987). Retain, but also reclaim, modernity, recognizing that its project can only be fulfilled in a utopian stage I call the slowmodern. Fast and slow, modern and premodern, blur to the point of identity. Technologies will serve human needs, people will pursue projects that define and enrich them, their children will be allowed to find their ways, and people will be at one with their bodies.

References

Adorno, Theodor W. 1945. "A Social Critique of Radio Music." *Kenyon Review* 9:208–17.

1954. "How to Look at Television." *Quarterly of Film, Radio and Television* 3:213–35.

1973. *Negative Dialectics.* New York: Seabury.

1978. *Minima Moralia.* London: Verso.

1984. *Aesthetic Theory.* London: Routledge and Kegan Paul.

Adorno, Theodor W., Else Frenkel-Brunswik, Daniel Levinson, and R. N. Sanford. 1950. *The Authoritarian Personality.* New York: Harper.

Agger, Ben. 1989a. *Fast Capitalism: A Critical Theory of Significance.* Urbana: University of Illinois Press.

1989b. *Reading Science: A Literary, Political and Sociological Analysis.* Dix Hills, N.Y.: General Hall.

1990. *The Decline of Discourse: Reading, Writing and Resistance in Postmodern Capitalism.* London: Falmer Press.

1992a. *Cultural Studies as Critical Theory.* London: Falmer Press.

1992b. *The Discourse of Domination: From Critical Theory to Postmodernism.* Evanston, Ill.: Northwestern University Press.

1993. *Gender, Culture and Power: Toward a Feminist Postmodern Critical Theory.* Westport, Conn.: Praeger.

2000. *Public Sociology: From Social Facts to Literary Acts.* Lanham, Md.: Rowman & Littlefield.

2002. *Postponing the Postmodern: Sociological Practices, Selves and Theories.* Lanham, Md.: Rowman & Littlefield.

2004. *The Virtual Self: A Contemporary Sociology.* Boston: Blackwell.

Althusser, Louis. 1970. *For Marx.* London: Allen Lane.

Aronowitz, Stanley. 1988. *Science as Power: Discourse and Ideology in Modern Society.* Minneapolis: University of Minnesota Press.

1992. *False Promises,* 2nd ed. Durham, N.C.: Duke University Press.

Baudrillard, Jean. 1983. *Simulations.* New York: Semiotext(e).

———. 1988. *America.* London: Verso.

Baumgardner, Jennifer, and Amy Richards. 2000. *Manifesta: Young Women, Feminism, and the Future.* New York: Farrar, Straus and Giroux.

Bay, Christian. 1958. *The Structure of Freedom.* Palo Alto, Calif.: Stanford University Press.

Beauvoir, Simone de. 1953. *The Second Sex.* New York: Knopf.

Bell, Daniel. 1960. *The End of Ideology.* Glencoe, Ill.: Free Press.

———. 1973. *The Coming of Post-Industrial Society.* New York: Basic.

Bendix, Reinhard. 1956. *Work and Authority in Industry: Ideologies of Management in the Course of Industrialization.* New York: Wiley.

Benjamin, Walter. 1999. *The Arcades Project.* Cambridge, Mass.: Harvard University Press.

Blumstein, Philip, and Pepper Schwartz. 1983. *American Couples: Money, Work, Sex.* New York: Pocket.

Bordo, Susan. 1993. *Unbearable Weight: Feminism, Western Culture and the Body.* Berkeley: University of California Press.

Borradori, Giovanna. 2003. *Philosophy in a Time of Terror: Dialogues with Jürgen Habermas and Jacques Derrida.* Chicago: University of Chicago Press.

Bourdieu, Pierre. 1998. *On Television.* New York: New Press.

Bowles, Samuel, and Herbert Gintis. 1976. *Schooling in Capitalist America.* New York: Basic.

Braverman, Harry. 1974. *Labor and Monopoly Capital: The Degradation of Work in the Twentieth Century.* New York: Monthly Review Press.

Brodkey, Linda. 1987. *Academic Writing as Social Practice.* Philadelphia: Temple University Press.

Chodorow, Nancy. 1978. *The Reproduction of Mothering.* Berkeley: University of California Press.

Coupland, Douglas. 1991. *Generation X: Tales from an Accelerated Culture.* New York: St. Martin's.

Cowan, Ruth Schwartz. 1985. *More Work for Mother: The Ironies of Household Technology, from the Open Hearth to the Microwave.* New York: Basic.

dalla Costa, Mariarosa, and Selma James. 1973. *The Power of Women and the Subversion of the Community.* Bristol, U.K.: Falling Wall Press.

Davis, Mike. 1990. *City of Quartz: Excavating the Future in Los Angeles.* London: Verso.

DeGrazia, Sebastian. 1962. *Of Time, Work and Leisure.* New York: Twentieth Century Fund.

Dellasega, Cheryl. 2001. *Surviving Ophelia: Mothers Share Their Wisdom in Navigating the Tumultuous Teenage Years.* New York: Ballantine.

References

Derrida, Jacques. 1976. *Of Grammatology*. Baltimore: Johns Hopkins University Press.

Durkheim, Émile. 1956. *The Division of Labor in Society*. Glencoe, Ill.: Free Press.

Dyer-Witheford, Nick. 1999. *Cyber-Marx: Cycles and Circuits of Struggle in High Technology Capitalism*. Urbana: University of Illinois Press.

Ehrenreich, Barbara. 1983. *The Hearts of Men: American Dreams and the Flight from Commitment*. Garden City, N.Y.: Anchor Press/Doubleday.

———. 2001. *Nickel and Dimed: On (Not) Getting By in America*. New York: Metropolitan Books.

Eisenstein, Zillah, ed. 1979. *Capitalist Patriarchy and the Case for Socialist Feminism*. New York: Monthly Review Press.

Ewen, Stuart. 1976. *Captains of Consciousness: Advertising the Social Roots of the Consumer Culture*. New York: McGraw-Hill.

Foucault, Michel. 1977. *Discipline and Punish*. New York: Pantheon.

Friedan, Betty. 1963. *The Feminine Mystique*. New York: Norton.

Garfinkel, Harold. 1967. *Studies in Ethnomethodology*. Englewood Cliffs, N.J.: Prentice-Hall.

Gergen, Kenneth. 2000. *The Saturated Self: Dilemmas of Identity in Contemporary Life*. New York: Basic.

Gitlin, Todd. 2003. *Letters to a Young Activist*. New York: Basic.

Gordon, Avery. 1997. *Ghostly Matters: Haunting and the Sociological Imagination*. Minneapolis: University of Minnesota Press.

———. 2004. *Keeping Good Time: Reflections on Knowledge, Power and People*. Boulder, Colo.: Paradigm Publishers.

Gottdiener, Mark. 1997. *The Theming of America: Dreams, Visions and Commercial Spaces*. Boulder, Colo.: Westview Press.

Gramsci, Antonio. 1971. *Selections from the Prison Notebooks*. London: Lawrence and Wishart.

Gurstein, Penelope. 1991. *Wired to the World, Chained to the Home: Telework in Daily Life*. Vancouver: University of British Columbia Press.

Habermas, Jürgen. 1984. *The Theory of Communicative Action*, vol. 1. Boston: Beacon.

———. 1987a. *The Philosophical Discourse of Modernity*. Cambridge, Mass.: MIT Press.

———. 1987b. *The Theory of Communicative Action*, vol. 2. Boston: Beacon.

Hardt, Michael, and Antonio Negri. 2000. *Empire*. Cambridge, Mass.: Harvard University Press.

Harvey, David. 1989. *The Condition of Postmodernity*. Oxford: Blackwell.

Hayden, Tom. 1962. *The Port Huron Statement of the Students for a Democratic Society*. www.orlok.com/tribe/insiders/huron.html.

Heidegger, Martin. 1962. *Being and Time*. New York: Harper.

171

Hersch, Patricia. 1998. *A Tribe Apart: A Journey into the Heart of American Adolescence*. Ballantine: New York.

Hesse-Biber, Sharlene. 1996. *Am I Thin Enough Yet? The Cult of Thinness and the Commercialization of Identity*. New York: Harper and Row.

Hochschild, Arlie. 1989. *The Second Shift*. New York: Viking.

Hofstadter, Richard. 1963. *Anti-Intellectualism in American Life*. New York: Knopf.

Holmes, Douglas R. 2000. *Integral Europe: Fast-Capitalism, Multiculturalism, Neofascism*. Princeton, N.J.: Princeton University Press.

Horkheimer, Max. 1974. *Eclipse of Reason*. New York: Seabury.

Horkheimer, Max, and Theodor W. Adorno. 1972. *Dialectic of Enlightenment*. New York: Herder and Herder.

Huyssen, Andreas. 1986. *After the Great Divide: Modernism, Mass Culture, Postmodernism*. Bloomington: Indiana University Press.

Jacoby, Russell. 1975. *Social Amnesia: A Critique of Conformist Psychology from Adler to Laing*. Boston: Beacon Press.

1987. *The Last Intellectuals: American Culture in the Age of Academe*. New York: Basic.

Jaggar, Alison. 1983. *Feminist Politics and Human Nature*. Totowa, N.J.: Rowman and Allanheld.

Jameson, Fredric. 1991. *Postmodernism, or, the Cultural Logic of Late Capitalism*. Durham, N.C.: Duke University Press.

Jay, Martin. 1973. *The Dialectical Imagination*. Boston: Little, Brown.

Kay, Jane Holtz. 1997. *Asphalt Nation: How the Automobile Took Over America, and How We Can Take It Back*. New York: Crown.

Kellner, Douglas. 1995. *Media Culture: Cultural Studies, Identity and Politics between the Modern and the Postmodern*. New York: Routledge.

2003. *From 9/11 to Terror War: The Dangers of the Bush Legacy*. Lanham, Md.: Rowman & Littlefield.

Kralovec, Etta, and John Buell. 2000. *The End of Homework: How Homework Disrupts Families, Overburdens Children and Limits Learning*. Boston: Beacon.

Lasch, Christopher. 1977. *Haven in a Heartless World: The Family Besieged*. New York: Basic.

Levine, Mel. 2002. *A Mind at a Time*. New York: Simon and Schuster.

Lukács, Georg. 1971. *History and Class Consciousness*. London: Merlin.

Luke, Timothy W. 1989. *Screens of Power: Ideology, Domination and Resistance in the Informational Society*. Evanston: University of Illinois Press.

forthcoming. *Virtual Ecologies: Social Order and Political Power in Cyberspace*. London: Sage.

Lyotard, Jean-François. 1984. *The Postmodern Condition: A Report on Knowledge*. Minneapolis: University of Minnesota Press.

MacKinnon, Catharine. 1988. *Pornography and Civil Rights*. Minneapolis: University of Minnesota Press.

172

References

1993. *Only Words*. Cambridge, Mass.: Harvard University Press.

Mailer, Norman. 2003. *The Spooky Art: Some Thoughts on Writing*. New York: Random House.

Marcuse, Herbert. 1955. *Eros and Civilization*. New York: Vintage.

1960. *Reason and Revolution: Hegel and the Rise of Social Theory,* preface to the 2nd ed. Boston: Beacon.

1964. *One-Dimensional Man*. Boston: Beacon.

Marx, Karl. 1964. *Early Writings*. Edited by Tom Bottomore. New York: McGraw-Hill.

1967. *Capital: A Critique of Political Economy*. New York: International Publishers.

Marx, Karl, and Friedrich Engels. 1947. *The German Ideology*. New York: International Publishers.

1967. *The Communist Manifesto*. New York: Pantheon.

Merleau-Ponty, Maurice. 1964a. *Sense and Non-Sense*. Evanston, Ill.: Northwestern University Press.

1964b. *Signs*. Evanston, Ill.: Northwestern University Press.

Miller, James. 1987. "Democracy Is in the Streets." In *From Port Huron to the Siege of Chicago*. New York: Simon and Schuster.

Miller, Mark Crispin. 1988. *Boxed In: The Culture of TV*. Evanston, Ill.: Northwestern University Press.

Mills, C. Wright. 1951. *White Collar*. New York: Oxford University Press.

Negroponte, Nicholas. 1996. *Being Digital*. New York: Knopf.

O'Neill, John. 1972. *Sociology as a Skin Trade*. New York: Harper and Row.

1985. *Five Bodies: The Human Shape of Modern Society*. Ithaca, N.Y.: Cornell University Press.

Parsons, Talcott. 1951. *The Social System*. New York: Free Press.

Petrini, Carlo. 2003. *Slow Food: The Case for Taste*. New York: Columbia University Press.

Poster, Mark. 1975. *Existential Marxism in Postwar France: From Sartre to Althusser*. Princeton, N.J.: Princeton University Press.

1990. *The Mode of Information*. Chicago: University of Chicago Press.

2001. *What's the Matter with the Internet?* Minneapolis: University of Minnesota Press.

Pritikin, Nathan. 1979. *The Pritikin Program for Diet and Exercise*. New York: Bantam.

Ritzer, George. 1993. *The McDonaldization of Society*. Newbury Park, Calif.: Pine Forge.

Rodgers, Bill. 1980. *Marathoning*. New York: Simon and Schuster.

Rorty, Richard. 1997. *Truth, Politics and "Post-Modernism."* Assen, Netherlands: Van Gorcum.

Ryan, Michael. 1982. *Marxism and Deconstruction*. Baltimore: Johns Hopkins University Press.

Ryan, Michael, and Douglas Kellner. 1988. *Camera Politica: The Politics and Ideology of Contemporary Hollywood Film.* Bloomington: Indiana University Press.

Sartre, Jean-Paul. 1956. *Being and Nothingness.* New York: Philosophical Library.

1976. *Critique of Dialectical Reason.* London: New Left Books.

Schlosser, Eric. 2001. *Fast Food Nation: The Dark Side of the All-American Meal.* Boston: Houghton Mifflin.

2003. *Reefer Madness: Sex, Drugs and Cheap Labor in the American Black Market.* Boston: Houghton Mifflin.

Schumacher, E. F. 1973. *Small Is Beautiful: A Study of Economics as If People Mattered.* New York: Harper and Row.

Sennett, Richard. 1977. *The Fall of Public Man.* New York: Knopf.

Sheehan, George. 1978. *Running and Being.* New York: Simon and Schuster.

Shorter, Edward. 1975. *The Making of the Modern Family.* New York: Basic.

Sloterdijk, Peter. 1987. *Critique of Cynical Reason.* Minneapolis: University of Minnesota Press.

Smith, Adam. 1998. *An Inquiry into the Nature and Causes of the Wealth of Nations.* New York: Oxford University Press.

Soja, Edward. 1989. *Postmodern Geographies: The Reassertion of Space in Critical Social Theory.* London: Verso.

Taylor, Frederick W. 1967. *The Principles of Scientific Management.* New York: Norton.

Turkle, Sherry. 1995. *Life on the Screen: Identity in the Age of the Internet.* New York: Simon and Schuster.

Walby, Sylvia. 1990. *Theorizing Patriarchy.* Oxford: Basil Blackwell.

Weber, Max. 1978. *Economy and Society: An Outline of Interpretive Sociology.* Berkeley: University of California Press.

Wiggershaus, Rolf. 1994. *The Frankfurt School: Its History, Theories and Political Significance.* Cambridge, Mass.: MIT Press.

Zaretsky, Eli. 1976. *Capitalism, the Family and Personal Life.* New York: Harper and Row.

Zerubavel, Eviatar. 1999. *The Clockwork Muse: A Practical Guide to Writing Theses, Dissertations and Books.* Cambridge, Mass.: Harvard University Press.

Index

Index

About the Author

Ben Agger is Professor of Sociology and Humanities at the University of Texas at Arlington, where he also directs the Center for Theory (www.uta.edu/center-for-theory) and edits the electronic journal *Fast Capitalism* (www.fastcapitalism.com). Agger has written extensively on critical theory and on cultural, media, and Internet studies. His recent books include *Postponing the Postmodern* and *The Virtual Self*. His next book, with Beth Anne Shelton, is entitled *Fast Families, Virtual Children* and develops themes addressed in *Speeding Up Fast Capitalism*. He is also planning a future project on the 1960s, generation, and identity.

DATE DUE